THE COST OF
FREEDOM

THE COST OF
FREEDOM

DR JAIMIE OLIVER GARANDE

The Cost of Freedom

First published in Great Britain in 2011. Re-Published in 2019 by My Destiny Inc. Publishing.

ISBN: 978-1-64669-302-3

My Destiny Inc. Publishing
Email: info@mydestinyinc.org

Tel: +44 (0) 207 164 6508
Fax: +44 (0) 207 681 3474

Book cover design and layout by Reach Publishing: www.wearereach.org

CONTENTS

Dedication vii

Introduction... ix

Chapter One   Understand the Original Blueprint........................... 1

Chapter Two   You have to pay the price 11

Chapter Three   Beware the vagaries of religious thinking............... 23

Chapter Four   There will be giants in your land 33

Chapter Five   Dare to Dream....................................... 47

Chapter Six   Study your Covenant! 55

Chapter Seven   Unstinting Dedication to God Is the Key............... 63

Chapter Eight   Sin makes minnows of men................................... 75

Chapter Nine   What do you stand for?... 85

Dedication

This book is dedicated to all the teachers of Gods Word who are committed to bringing true freedom to those they teach.

Introduction

'He has no form or comeliness, and when we see Him, there is no beauty that we should desire Him. He is despised and rejected by men, a Man of sorrows and acquainted with grief. And we hid, as it were, our faces from Him; He was despised, and we did not esteem Him.

Surely He has borne our griefs and carried our sorrows. Yet we esteemed Him stricken, smitten by God, and afflicted. But He was wounded for our transgressions, He was bruised for our iniquities. The chastisement for our peace was upon Him, and by His stripes we are healed.

All we like sheep have gone astray. We have turned, every one, to his own way. And the Lord has laid on Him the iniquity of us all. He was oppressed and He was afflicted, yet He opened not His mouth. He was led as a lamb to the slaughter, and as a sheep before its shearers is silent. So He opened not His mouth. He was taken from prison and from judgment, and who will declare His generation?

For He was cut off from the land of the living, for the transgressions of My people He was stricken. And they made His grave with the wicked, but with the rich at His death, because He had done no violence, nor was any deceit in His mouth.

Yet it pleased the Lord to bruise Him. He has put Him to grief. When You make His soul an offering for sin, He shall see His seed, He shall prolong His days, and the pleasure of the Lord shall prosper in His hand. He shall see the labour of His soul, and be satisfied. By His knowledge My righteous Servant shall justify many, for He shall bear their iniquities. Therefore I will divide Him a portion with the great, and He shall divide the spoil with the strong, because He poured out His soul unto death, and He was numbered with the transgressors. And He bore the sin of many, and made intercession for the transgressors. (Isaiah 53)

Dr Jaimie Oliver Garande

I was eight years old when I first watched the film *Jesus of Nazareth*. I can still vividly recall the feelings of horror and fear I felt as I witnessed Jesus being mercilessly whipped, spat on, violently abused and then brutally crucified, enduring a level of pain and suffering that is simply unimaginable. It marked me forever, and for many years I flat out refused to watch anything that would remind me of the unbridled savagery of that world changing event.

Twenty seven years later, I still marvel at the gruesome death that our Saviour endured. It remains the single most selfless act ever performed by an individual in the entire history of the world. I must admit, I still hate watching any dramatisations of it. Even Mel Gibson's critically acclaimed *The Passion of the Christ* received a single reluctant viewing. But whenever I do, it merely helps to reinforce the feelings of gratitude I feel, knowing that everything He endured, He endured for me.

It cost Jesus everything He had to purchase our freedom at Calvary. He stripped Himself of His royalty, made Himself of no reputation, and was sacrificed on a manmade cross. He was beaten to a pulp, and so disfigured in the process that you could hardly make out His features. We will never truly comprehend this side of eternity, just how much He suffered.

But He was willing to go through it all, because He knew that this was the only way to redeem a fallen world of men and women, many of whom were totally oblivious to their need for salvation. He recognized that only through His selfless death would eternal life become available to all who accepted Him. If there was any other way to pay the penalty for our sin then God would have chosen it. But there really wasn't. Only Jesus qualified as the sinless, spotless Son of God, and only Jesus had the credentials necessary to provide a pure, unblemished sacrifice.

On the 13th of September 1995 I accepted Him as my Lord and Saviour and experienced feelings of freedom and liberty that are totally unique to this life changing experience. But it has taken me all of the subsequent fifteen years to even begin to scratch the surface of the true nature of the redemption that was purchased for me on that fateful day, over 2000 years ago.

Consequently I have made it my primary assignment in the time that I have left on the earth to ensure that I get to grips with, truly understand, and then maximise all of the privileges and benefits that Jesus died for me to receive. I figure that is the greatest honour that I can accord Him. I am also committed to making sure that as many people as possible do the exact same thing.

It is tragic to see how often we have been deceived into accepting so much less than the full extent of our inheritance. Formal, lifeless and empty religion will tell you that God is only interested in your needs and not your wants. It will tell you that you should be grateful for what you have and stop trying to aim for more because when you do so it just shows that you are greedy and carnal. It will encourage you to put up with sickness in your body by convincing you that it is God's will for you to be unwell, and that somehow He gets a macabre satisfaction from seeing you suffer before He decides to heal you. It will convince you that poverty will bring you closer to God when it will have exactly the opposite effect. It will convince you to be content with scraping the bottom of the barrel in this life, and yet somehow make you believe that you qualify for the best that heaven has to offer when you die.

But a living, vibrant relationship with God will quickly make you realize the awesomeness of your salvation package, and the best way you can show your heartfelt appreciation for His selfless generosity is to become everything He said you could become, and have everything He said you could have.

Our salvation was free to us, but it certainly cost Jesus everything He had. Making the decision to maximise our freedoms in Him will cost us in turn. We will be misunderstood, maligned and ridiculed. We will be criticized, despised and berated. This shouldn't surprise us, because it is easier to follow the path of least resistance and be average and mediocre, than it is to step out in faith and become truly great. Salvation is free, but enjoying all of its benefits will cost you everything you've got.

There are so many areas of our lives where we tolerate bondage and slavery and we don't even realize that in doing so we are living contrary to our covenant with God and our accompanying inheritance in Christ. But regardless of the cost to us personally, we have to be willing to do whatever it takes to eliminate that bondage. God wouldn't have it any other way.

My entire life philosophy can be summed up thus: "*The will of God for your life will not happen in spite of you, but because of you.*" There is no question that God wants you free—He has demonstrated His commitment to this unequivocally. But just because He wants you free doesn't mean you will experience freedom. You still have your part to play.

This book is all about the cost of freedom to you. In life nothing worth having will simply fall into your lap. We also have a rabid adversary who will do everything in his power to resist your attempts to experience freedom on the God level.

My prayer is that as you read this book it will inspire you to reach out and receive every single part of your heavenly inheritance. You have got to realize that your life as you know it is not the definition of what it can be. There is so much more for you to become. Decide today to pay the price to find out what belongs to you. Believe me it will be worth it.

Dr. Jaimie Oliver Garande

Chapter One

UNDERSTAND THE ORIGINAL BLUEPRINT

"You seen how a man was made a slave: you shall see how a slave was made a man."

Frederck Douglass

At the heart of international political theory lies a much debated but often misunderstood ideal known as self determination. At its most basic it refers to the right of individual nations to freely determine their affairs without the interference of outsiders. It is a very necessary tenet, because without it no country would be able to decide the political, social and economic direction it took. Its story would simply be one of constant deference to the whims of the more powerful nations around it.

But the right to self determination doesn't just have application at the national and international level. It goes to the core of every human relationship. It is the same thinking that was behind the phrase *'life, health, liberty or possessions'* as espoused by John Locke, or its later equivalent, *'life, liberty and pursuit of happiness'* as contained in the US Declaration of Independence. Every man and woman has an innate knowledge of their right to freely determine the course of their lives.

And with good reason. Our original right to chart our own course in life was a God given mandate. That's why every man born since Adam knows instinctively that he was created to be free, and has an attendant awareness of his responsibility to dominate his environment and not be dominated by anything or anyone.

'Then God said, "Let Us make man in Our image, according to Our likeness; let them have dominion over the fish of the sea, over the

birds of the air, and over the cattle, over all the earth and over every creeping thing that creeps on the earth.'" (Genesis 1:26)

Man was given complete authority over the earth around him. That authority did not extend however to the imposition of his will on his fellow human beings. Tragically, the history of the world has seen the forced implementation of a varying number of draconian and exploitative systems on the weak by the strong. From the unfortunate oppression of feudalism to the unparalleled brutality of slavery, right through to the inexcusable excesses of colonialism, men have tried to impose their will on others for their personal gain. Even in the twenty first century, the existence of modern day sweat shops and the vagaries of human trafficking are evidence of man's insatiable penchant for dominating his fellow human beings.

And for the longest time all of those systems seem to work. Great economies were built on the back of the unimaginable cruelty of the Roman Empire or the unbridled savagery of the American and British slave masters. But without fail, each of these seemingly invincible political animals experienced, and in some cases continue to experience the negative consequences of their oppressive regimes. Those involved in creating the systems did not understand the basic flaws that were inherent in each of the systems. That each carried within itself the seeds of its own destruction. Men are able to put up with oppression for a while but eventually they become aware of their intrinsic value and true essence, and will fight to recapture their lost glory.

When a man isn't free, he is a mere shadow of his true self. He cowers in the face of adversity, accomplishes little of significance in his life, and contents himself with acquiring a few trinkets during his time on the earth. He endures the drudgery of his life, hating himself more and more with each passing day, knowing deep down that there has to be more to life than this depressing cycle.

"Any existence deprived of freedom is a kind of death."

Gen Michael Aoun

When God created Adam and Eve, they were created to live forever. The perfect man and woman, in perfect harmony with their environment. They were never meant to experience death, or the ravages of sickness and disease. They were never designed to have to put up with bondage, depression, stress and disappointment. Instead they were to spend eternity extending God's creative work in the earth and in the other galaxies that He had made. God's original design was for man to exercise dominion in the earth and subdue the devil if and when he tried to cause further insurrection.

Adam was placed in a unique position above all of nature. He alone among all forms of life was made in God's image. In God's plan, we as human beings were placed at the top of a hierarchy of creation, with a divine mandate to rule it in partnership with Him.

But from the moment Adam committed high treason and handed over his birthright to the devil, he became a hapless victim of the very thing he had been in control of previously:

> *"Cursed is the ground because of you; through painful toil you will eat of it all the days of your life. It will produce thorns and thistles for you, and you will eat the plants of the field. By the sweat of your brow you will eat your food . . ." (Genesis 3:17-19)*

Even making a living became difficult. Instead of enjoying his work and experiencing fruitfulness and productivity, working became a chore and produced minimal results. Man would slave away but would find himself caught up in a vicious cycle of diminishing returns.

Man was also cursed to die. God had always intended for man to live forever, but Adam and Eve's sin scuppered heaven's original plan.

> *"By the sweat of your brow you will eat your food until you return to the ground, since from it you were taken; for dust you are and to dust you will return." (v19)*

On top of all that, Adam also became cannon fodder for the enemy. He was cursed to return to the dust, and the devil was cursed to feed on that very same dust.

> *'So the Lord God said to the serpent, "Because you have done this, cursed are you above all the livestock and all the wild animals. You will crawl on your belly and you will eat dust all the days of your life." (v14)*

The next four thousand years of human history were an interesting mix of some incredible highs and some very terrible lows. From the time that Adam fell, God immediately instituted a plan of redemption that would result in man being able to recapture his former glory. Many men and women were born and used by God to bring a temporal release from the woes that His people were experiencing. From Moses to Gideon, and Samson to David, they all began the process of delivering God's people from oppression. In Moses' case:

> *'The Lord said, "I have surely seen the affliction of My people who are in Egypt, and have given heed to their cry because of their taskmasters, for I am aware of their sufferings. Therefore come now and I will send you to Pharaoh so that you may bring My people, the sons of Israel out of Egypt"'. (Exodus 3:7,10)*

God told Gideon:

> *"Go in this your strength and deliver Israel from the hand of Midian. Have I not sent you?" (Judges 6:14)*

And to Samson's parents He said:

> *"For behold, you shall conceive and bear a son. And no razor shall come upon his head, for the child shall be a Nazirite to God from the womb; and he shall begin to deliver Israel out of the hand of the Philistines." (Judges 13:5)*

All of these faith giants began the process of liberating their brothers and sisters from captivity, but that is all they could do. They couldn't complete the process because true freedom would only come at the hands of Jesus, whose express aim in coming to the earth was to deliver men from everything that was trying to keep them in any form of bondage.

> *"The Spirit of the Lord is upon Me, because He has anointed Me to preach the gospel to the poor; He has sent Me to heal the broken-hearted, to proclaim liberty to the captives and recovery of sight to the blind, to set at liberty those who are oppressed; To proclaim the acceptable year of the Lord." (Luke 4:18-19)*

Jesus' express mandate was to restore us to who we were at the very beginning. That meant destroying every single one of the works of the devil and eliminating bondage wherever it existed.

> *'But unto every one of us is given grace according to the measure of the gift of Christ. Wherefore he saith, When he ascended up on high, he led captivity captive, and gave gifts unto men. (Now that he ascended, what is it but that he also descended first into the lower parts of the earth? He that descended is the same also that ascended up far above all heavens, that he might fill all things.) (Ephesians 4:7-10)*

The freedom God has made available to us is very real. Regardless of whatever form of bondage you may be in, His power is available today to deliver you from it. It certainly doesn't matter how long you have been in bondage. The power of God is no less powerful because of the passage of time. When you consider the work Jesus accomplished on the Cross, its intent was to restore us to our original standing in Eden, and then to enable us to fulfil the assignment that Adam left incomplete.

> *'Christ purchased our freedom, redeeming us from the curse of the Law and its condemnation by Himself becoming a curse for us, for it is written in the Scriptures, Cursed is everyone who hangs on a tree, to*

5

> *the end that through their receiving Christ Jesus, the blessing promised to Abraham might come upon the Gentiles, so that we through faith might all receive the realization of the promise of the Holy Spirit.' (Galatians 3:13-14)*

Instead of buying into the lie that life is a drag and that our aim in life should be to submissively put up with life's difficulties until we enjoy the sweet respite that is offered by death, you ought instead to realize that notwithstanding the very real challenges that you may encounter, there is a new level of living available to you in God. But you are going to have to search it out diligently so that you can enjoy it fully. Because Jesus literally put his neck on the line for you, you can live everyday in the knowledge that your story has changed from one of dismal defeat and failure to one of enduring success.

> *Jesus said, "I tell you most solemnly that anyone who chooses a life of sin is trapped in a dead-end life and is, in fact, a slave. A slave is a transient, who can't come and go at will. The Son, though, has an established position, the run of the house. So if the Son sets you free, you are free through and through."' (John 8:36)*

Don't be fooled into believing that all God wants to do is prescribe a long list of rules for you to obey so that he can restrict your freedoms and liberties. Naturally, He does want you to avoid the temporary pleasure of sin, because for all that it promises, sin in the final analysis will only serve to enslave you. And you and I were never created to be slaves to anything or anyone. God wants you to be in practical control of every area of your environment, reigning as the king or queen that you were originally created to be.

> *'For if, by the trespass of the one man, death reigned through that one man, how much more will those who receive God's abundant provision of grace and of the gift of righteousness reign in life through the one man, Jesus Christ.' (Romans 5:17)*

God put man in charge of the entire world. That included the animals, the vegetation and the elements. For us to be in the place today where we allow ourselves to be enslaved by processed herbs, or where we are subject to a never ending list of phobias and addictions must make Him look at us in genuine amazement. That was never His original intention. And today as you read this book, I join my faith with yours and declare that from this day forward you will no longer be held captive by the things that you should be controlling. You are free now in Jesus' name!

> *"What is man, that you keep him in mind? the son of man, that you take him into account?" (Psalm 8:4)*

I can talk authoritatively about the delivering and restorative power of Jesus' blood, because like many of you I have experienced it firsthand. When I was at university I spent a large part of my time on campus partying and really living it up in one night club or another. It seemed like I was having the time of my life, until the day when I woke up and I realized that I was fast becoming an alcoholic. One evening I looked into my wallet and realized that I only had $4 which could have either bought me a meal or a beer. Sadly, I chose the beer. Up to that point I had laughed off suggestions that I had a problem. But that was my wake up call. I made a decision there and then to do away with my drinking which had gotten way out of control.

The only problem was that much like the New Year's resolutions that everyone has made at one point or another, the spirit was willing, but the flesh was incredibly weak. It wasn't long before I was back doing what I had been doing before, and feeling absolutely awful every time I fell off the wagon. I knew I needed help, but I wasn't sure where to turn.

> *'By strength shall no man prevail.' (1 Samuel 2:9)*

Fast forward two weeks and I found myself in an evening church service on the university campus. Someone had told me that they had a visiting speaker in, and I figured it would be better to go and check it out rather than mope around in my room since I didn't have any money to go out. I stepped into the chapel and couldn't help but notice the somewhat odd stares that I was getting from some of the regulars. I wasn't dressed like anyone else, what with my two earrings, my ridiculously (in hindsight) baggy jeans and my Caterpillar boots making me stand out like a sore thumb but I didn't let it bother me.

I don't really remember what the preacher taught on that night. What I do remember however, was him inviting those who were not saved to give their lives to the Lord. He also invited those who were experiencing bondage in their lives to come and receive a complete release. As much as I didn't want to, I found myself running up to the front and throwing my hands in the air. I also remember the preacher telling all the people gathered at the front of that small room that if we wanted to receive Holy Spirit baptism we could get that too. I had always been rather sceptical about the whole speaking in tongues 'thing' because I had heard people speaking in tongues before and it all seemed rather strange and contrived. But as I stood there and repeated the sinners' prayer, together with some other people who had come up with me, I felt a strange glow go all over me, and I felt so full of joy I could hardly bear it. Incredibly, I began to speak in an unknown tongue at the same time, and was so overwhelmed by the whole experience I thought I would collapse. As soon as the service was over I ran to a payphone and called my wife Nyarai. I was gushing. I had been set free and I knew it.

I tried once after that to binge drink, because I wanted to know if this salvation stuff really worked. It was never the same again. I had lost the desire for the thing that had become such an important part of my life. The bondage was completely gone.

I know that not everyone's salvation story is the same. Some are a lot more dramatic than mine, others less so. I also know that the deliverance that God has made freely available to us may require us to work it out over a longer period of time. I have had areas in my life where I have had to work through certain issues for years, but the freedom I have subsequently enjoyed has been no less real.

There is someone reading this book right now that is bound in an area of their lives and it seems like there is no way out for you. The devil specialises in convincing you that you are the only one in that particular predicament and in making the shame of your sin overwhelm you. But the truth is that you may not have been born free, but you can certainly be born again and go free! Let the supernatural power of God deliver you today from every form of satanic bondage!

In his letter to the church at Galatia, as Paul writes to exhort them not to allow legalism and a religious spirit to override the vibrancy of their relationship with God, he makes a powerful statement:

> *"It was for freedom that Christ set us free; therefore keep standing firm and do not be subject again to a yoke of slavery." (Galatians 5:1)*

This statement has become one of the cornerstones of my individual walk and that of our church as we journey towards our destiny in God.

Jesus came to set us free. No reality is bigger than this one. Our responsibility therefore is to make sure that we stand firm on the basis of that knowledge, and do not take ourselves back into slavery by our own hand. Slavery is a yoke. It will take you to places you do not want to go, and charge you a price you cannot pay. In this season of your life I want to encourage you to locate your freedom in Christ and then decide to hold on to it no matter what it costs you. Jesus did His part. It's time for you to do yours.

When God created Adam He was designed to be irresistible. He had a phenomenal mind that didn't know such words as *impossible* or phrases like *it can't be done*. He never fell sick, or felt like he had no options in life. He was never created to live in one corner of the world when the whole world lay before him as a blank, unexplored canvas. He was never designed to speak words of defeat and despondency. He was an awesome specimen, untainted by fear and self-doubt.

When Adam walked the earth He reflected the essence of who God was in every imaginable way. Like God, whatever he called a thing, that was its name. He had a limitless mind and had the capacity to come up with names for the millions of different species of creature that wandered the earth. It is often said that the English language has over 250,000 words. The average person on the other hand knows only 400 of them, and they make up the difference by swearing. That would mean that if someone like that had to name all of the animals in the world, including all the sub-species, it wouldn't be long before they would run out of words and today we would have over 1000 animals with the same name!

Adam certainly wasn't intended to ever be short of ideas. He was the perfect man in perfect control of himself and his environment and in perfect union with his Creator.

Early church father St Irenaeus wrote, *"Man fully alive is the glory of God."* God's greatest desire, contrary to public opinion and sentiment, is to see man functioning at his optimum level, enjoying life, in control of his surroundings, and not a hapless victim of happenstance. When he looks upon your life, He wants to see you restored to the reality of what Adam experienced before he fell.

> *"And so it is written,"* The first man Adam became a living being. *"The last Adam became a life-giving spirit."* (1 Corinthians 15:45)

Now through the sacrificial death, burial and resurrection of Jesus, it is possible for you and I to experience a level of living that most men will simply never enjoy, unless they tap into the grace of God and the redemptive power of God for themselves. You don't have to die before you can begin to experience freedom. Make the decision today to get everything that belongs to you, by understanding that it is available to you right now!

Chapter Two

YOU HAVE TO PAY THE PRICE

*"Freedom is never voluntarily given by the oppressor;
it must be demanded by the oppressed."*

Martin Luther King Jr.

Sir Isaac Newton's First Law of Motion, also called the Law of Inertia, states that *any object which is at rest will remain at rest unless acted on by an unbalanced force.* Unless an external force is applied to a stationary object it simply will not move.

Similarly, nothing will change in your life until you apply the force of faith to it. You can hope that it will change, believe that it will change, or even wish that it will change, but unless you actively do something about it, it simply will not change.

Years in the Christian faith have convinced me that too large a percentage of Believers have abdicated responsibility for their lives and bizarrely chosen to believe that if they are to enjoy any of God's promises, then God will have to make it happen, whilst they casually look on, with absolutely no effort on their part. That is simply not true. Even when God has promised you an inheritance you still need to fight and possess it:

> *"Rise, take your journey, and cross over the River Arnon. Look I have given into your hand Sihon the Amorite, king of Heshbon, and his land. Begin to possess it, and engage him in battle." (Deuteronomy 2:24)*

Picture this familiar scenario. God has just delivered the children of Israel from 400 years of captivity in Egypt through an awe inspiring demonstration of His power. The Israelites have ransacked their former captors treasure chests and left Egypt rejoicing. Life has never felt so good! Not only are they free, but they are loaded too! Could it possibly get better than this?

But first let me cast your mind back to the events that preceded their exodus out of Egypt. When Moses went to Pharaoh to request that he allow them to leave, he was unwavering in his commitment to enforcing their captivity.

> *'And afterward Moses and Aaron came and said to Pharaoh, "Thus says the Lord, the God of Israel, 'Let My people go that they may celebrate a feast to Me in the wilderness'". But Pharaoh said, "Who is the Lord that I should obey his voice to let Israel go? I do not know the Lord, and besides I will not let Israel go."* (Exodus 5:1-2)

To further emphasise his displeasure at their cheek, he increased the heaviness of their labour, and in a portent of what was to come, the Israelites turned on Moses in anger. It is often the case that the very same people you are leading to freedom are the ones who will turn on you the moment the freedom process proves to be a little more elusive and demanding than they initially anticipated.

That temporary discomfort puts off a lot of people from pushing forward with their drive towards freedom. Many are attracted by the lure of not having a cap on how much they can earn and so they leave their dead end jobs and start the business of their dreams. But just a few months removed from the 'security' of their pay cheque, and faced with the types of challenges all entrepreneurs invariably have to face, they begin to fondly reminisce about what it was like to have a guaranteed income. They conveniently forget what drove them to leave in the first place.

Every surge towards a new level will involve a certain degree of pain. Ask any athlete, and they will tell you that at some point in pursuing their discipline, they hit an invisible wall where it seems like they will have to throw in the towel. But incredibly, just beyond that wall is a sweet place called 'the second wind' where they feel reenergised and recharged and they are then able to press on towards their target. Don't allow the pain to cause you to go back and submit yourself to the very thing you despised so much.

Freedom always comes at great cost. Most people wish they had more money, a better life, a better education and better prospects, but they are often unwilling to take the necessary steps to make that a reality. Instead they remind themselves of the good old days, which incidentally were never as good as they make them out to be.

Once in the wilderness, the children of Israel began to cry out to Moses again.

> " . . . and the Israelites wept again and said, "Who will give us meat to eat? We remember the fish we ate freely in Egypt and without cost, the cucumbers, melons, leeks, onions, and garlic, but now our appetite is gone. There is nothing at all in the way of food to be seen but this manna." (Numbers 11:5-6)

The fish was free and without cost? I seem to recall it coming at a very heavy cost—they had lost their dignity, their creativity, their right to choose. Decisions were made for them, when by right they should have had the right to freely determine their affairs. They were content to have Pharaoh give them fish and never once realized that the one who controls the fish makes the rules. A rumbling stomach has caused many to give up their liberty. Just ask Esau who sold his birthright for a pot of beans.

But I am getting ahead of myself. Pharaoh would not let the children of Israel leave Egypt until he had no option but to free them. God had to force him into the place where he stopped reneging on his promises and constantly moving the goal posts. He didn't do it through protracted negotiation, but through an undeniable show of strength. Nothing less would do.

> 'Then the Lord said to Moses, "Yet I will bring one plague more on Pharaoh and on Egypt, afterwards he

> *will let you go. When he lets you go from here, he will thrust you out altogether."' (Exodus 11:1)*

> *"Now it came about at midnight that the Lord struck all the firstborn in the land of Egypt, from the firstborn of Pharaoh who sat on his throne to the firstborn of the captive who was in the dungeon, and all the firstborn of cattle. Pharaoh arose in the night, he and all his servants and all the Egyptians, and there was a great cry in Egypt for there was no home where there was not someone dead. Then he called for Moses and Aaron at night and said, "Rise up, get out from among my people, both you and the sons of Israel, and go worship the Lord as you have said."' (Exodus 12: 29-32)*

Freedom will never be given over freely. It must be enforced, not just once but continuously. Even after Pharaoh had allowed the Israelites to leave he had a sudden change of heart. Having enjoyed the benefits of free labour for so long, he was not about to relinquish those privileges without a fight.

Picture him as he gathers his well trained army and the best equipment possible, and decides to pursue and recapture their former slaves. As their chariots and horses thunder towards where the Israelites are gathered, the recently freed folk look back and see their former captors galloping towards them, intent on enslaving them once again.

Their hearts beating out of their chests, the Israelites begin to wail and remonstrate against Moses yet again.

> *'Then they said to Moses, "Is it because there were no graves in Egypt that you have taken us away to die in the wilderness? Why have you dealt with us in this way, bringing us out of Egypt? Is this not the word that we spoke to you in Egypt, saying, 'Leave us alone that we may serve the Egyptians'? For it would have been better for us to serve the Egyptians than to die in the wilderness."' (Exodus 14: 11-12)*

What a statement! Better to suffer in slavery than die for your freedom? How many times have we said something similar? I'd rather die in this dead end job than trust God and step out in faith knowing that I have so many other valuable contributions I could make to society. I'd rather make burial arrangements than believe that no matter how debilitating my sickness, God is willing and able to heal me. If you give up before you have even fought, what hope is there for you?

'If you faint in the day of battle, then you are a poor specimen.' (Proverbs 24:10)

"Those who desire to give up freedom in order to gain security will not have, nor do they deserve, either one." Benjamin Franklin

Now, please remember the children of Israel didn't have the luxury of reading the book of Exodus and knowing that God would part the Red Sea so that they could cross over on dry land. They were the book of Exodus! We have the benefit of knowing what happened. They didn't. So they tried looking up to God hoping He would do something. God's response is stirring:

'And the LORD said to Moses, "Why do you cry to Me? Tell the children of Israel to go forward. But lift up your rod, and stretch out your hand over the sea and divide it. And the children of Israel shall go on dry ground through the midst of the sea."' (Exodus 14:15)

The power of God is always at its most potent when we work together with Him. We do our part and then He is able to do His part. Expecting God to move without you moving is truly an exercise in futility. The covenant promises we are given always have a dual responsibility. We do our bit and then God does His. We tithe and He opens the windows of heaven for us. We plant and water and He provides the growth. We forgive, and He forgives us in turn. You make that job application and He gives you favour so that you get the position. You get the picture!

When Moses cooperated with God and stepped out in faith, the Children of Israel witnessed the greatest miracle they had ever seen—the Red Sea parted for them to cross over and then returned to drown Pharaoh and his army. What a victory! But it all stemmed from the power of divine cooperation—when God and man work together, tremendous things happen.

And let me remind you too that the devil is a lot like Pharaoh. Just because you have escaped his clutches once does not mean he will not be feverishly working to enslave you again. He will try over and over again to restore the status quo, where you are perennially under his feet. You and I will have to enforce our freedom continually.

> *"Behold, I have given you authority and power to trample upon serpents and scorpions, and physical and mental strength and ability over all the power that the enemy possesses, and nothing shall in any way harm you." (Luke 10:19)*

So even when the devil and his cronies start snooping around your stuff trying to rob you, your mission is to stamp out that insurrection the moment it begins. God told Adam:

> *"Be fruitful, multiply and fill the earth, and subdue it, using all its vast resources in the service of God and man, and have dominion over the fish of the sea, the birds of the air, and over every living creature that moves upon the earth." (Genesis 1:26)*

The Word 'subdue' is an interesting one. According to Webster's Dictionary, it means to *conquer and bring into subjection, to overpower by superior force, and to bring under mental or emotional control.* That means there will be so many things that will arise in our lives that have a spirit of insurrection resident in them, and our responsibility is to do whatever it takes to protect our freedom against them.

That means we can't afford to be lazy. We must be so diligent in our pursuit of total freedom, and eliminate any sort of laziness that tries to keep us average. There is always an incredibly high price to pay for freedom. Many feel the cost is too high. The truth is the cost is exactly the same—your life. You can either life live on your back in a show of abject laziness, or on your feet in committed pursuit of your goals, but you will be spending your life either way.

> *'The hand of the diligent shall bear rule, but the slothful shall be under tribute.' (Proverbs 12:24)*

Your financial situation isn't going to change just because you made a few confessions and spun yourself out of debt. You will have to apply yourself to understanding the laws that govern money and make a concerted effort to apply them to your situation until a change takes place. You aren't going to discover the reality of divine health sitting on your couch eating cupcakes and flicking the TV remote. There will always be a cost to pay for any sort of freedom, and the quicker you set about paying the price, the sooner you will be able to enjoy it.

> *"We must work the works of Him who sent Me as long as it is day; night is coming when no one can work."* *(John 9:4)*

All too often we have a basic mental level understanding of what it means to be free, but we put up with slavery in so many different forms that it makes a mockery of what we profess to know.

It is often said that when you don't pay for something you don't really appreciate it. Growing up, my parents would repeatedly tell us to switch off the lights in a room when we left it, or turn off the running tap water while we were brushing our teeth. We'd leave our toys outside and not think anything of it. Fast forward ten years and it was amazing how quickly I realized the importance of valuing what you pay for. I'm still trying to get my children to understand that lesson. Just like me, their time will come.

But not understanding the value of our freedom is often a product of immaturity. When you mature you value things more. Our freedom in Christ is the most awe inspiring gift we could ever have been given. All the money in the world wouldn't have been enough to pay for it. The moment we got born again it was freely given to us. Our new citizenship opened up a realm of possibility that was previously unimaginable. We ought to be eternally grateful.

> *The commander went to Paul and asked, "Tell me, are you a Roman citizen?" "Yes, I am," he answered. And the chief captain answered, With a great sum obtained I this freedom. And Paul said, but I was free born." (Acts 22:27-28)*

We already understand the power of citizenship. Being a citizen of a country allows you to benefit from certain privileges that are not available to people who aren't citizens. A British citizen is able to obtain advantages in the United Kingdom that American, Canadian, Russian or Nigerian citizens simply cannot enjoy. In much the same way, as a citizen of heaven, you and I have benefits and privileges that belong to us that we must take full advantage of.

> *"Blessed are those who wash their robes. They will be permitted to enter through the gates of the city and eat the fruit from the tree of life. Outside the city are the dogs—the sorcerers, the sexually immoral, the murderers, the idol worshipers, and all who love to live a lie." (Revelation 22:14-15)*

I wonder how much we would have been willing to pay for our heavenly citizenship if God had demanded such a payment. Maybe if we had paid a monetary price for it we would value it more. The things that are freely given to us by God have an inestimable value, but somehow because we forget that the price was paid for us, we think that they came cheap.

Being a parent myself I also understand all too well the frustrations of fellow parents who spend a fortune to educate their children and watch in exasperation as those children saunter casually through their time in school, blissfully unaware of the sacrifices that their parents have had to make to ensure that such an education is possible. But what a delight when you have a son or daughter who not only understands the extent of your sacrifice, but works to the very best of their ability to show their appreciation by getting excellent grades. You feel so very proud! That is exactly how God feels when we decide to maximise His sacrifice and build great lives for ourselves.

A few years ago in a time of prayer, The Lord spoke to me clearly and told me that it was impossible for a man to lead others to freedom until he was free himself. I took a long hard look at my life and realized that although I had visions of helping others to achieve freedom, there were so many areas of my life where I was in bondage and seemingly content to stay that way. From that day I set about to eliminate captivity in my life so that I could also help those who God assigned me to help. It included bondage to debt, the fear of being misunderstood, the fear of what my critics would have to say about me, and the fear to love unconditionally. It totally transformed my life.

> *"They promise them freedom, but they themselves are not free. They are slaves of things that will be destroyed. For people are slaves of anything that controls them."*
> *(2 Peter 2:18-20)*

Don't be surprised when you discover that there are people whose sole purpose in life is to shame you out of what belongs to you. They will ridicule your efforts from start to finish, and unless you get to the place where you have the strength of your convictions and can make decisions without having to have everyone agreeing with you, you will forever be a slave to public opinion. Have the guts to do what God tells you to do even when you know it won't go down well with everybody. Most of us don't make the decisions we need to make because we are afraid of how we will be perceived. And even when we do gather up the courage to make decisions we second guess ourselves no end. Peter J Daniels said something that changed me in that area permanently. He said, *"Successful people make decisions quickly and change them infrequently. Unsuccessful people make decisions slowly and they change them often."* Which camp do you fall in?

There are many folk who will promise freedom and liberty, but because their invitations are not based on the true freedom that only the Lord can provide, any such freedom is at once both fleeting and temporal.

> *"There used to be false prophets among God's people, just as you will have some false teachers in your group. They will secretly teach things that are wrong—teachings that will cause people to be lost. They will even refuse to accept the Master, Jesus, who bought their freedom. So they will bring quick ruin on themselves." (2 Peter 2:1)*

We are to partake in Christ's suffering. Not in the sense of going around looking for trouble and revelling in it, but rather in recognising that whenever you take a stand for the liberties that belong to you in Christ, tribulation will be an inevitable result. There will be those who will criticize and condemn you for what you believe. Others will ostracize you because their reality is totally different.

> *"Dear friends, don't be surprised at the fiery trials you are going through, as if something strange were happening to you. Instead, be very glad—for these trials make you partners with Christ in his suffering, so that you will have the wonderful joy of seeing his glory when it is revealed to all the world." (1 Peter 4:12-13)*

Nothing will change until you decide that you want it changed. History is replete with examples of men and women who were willing to challenge the status quo and pay the price to secure freedom from their oppressors.

On the 1st of December 1955 the diminutive Rosa Parks took a stand for equality that sparked a dramatic change in the laws governing racial relations in segregated America. On that landmark day the 42 year old Rosa refused to give up her seat as required by the infamous Jim Crow laws and the result was the Montgomery Bus Boycott that lasted for 381 days and resulted in the Supreme Court declaring segregation on transportation unconstitutional. In her own words: *"I would like to be remembered as a person who wanted to be free . . . so other people would be also free."* Later she was also quoted as saying, *"I have learned over the years that when one's mind is made up, this diminishes fear; knowing what must be done does away with fear."*

Mahatma Gandhi became the leader of the Indian nationalist movement and an international icon based on his non violent but committed focus on ensuring independence from British rule for the Indian people. His unstinting commitment to his cause inspired movements for civil rights and freedom across the world. He said *"I want freedom for the full expression of my personality."*

When you are in bondage, you are only half alive. Someone tells you what to eat, what to wear, where to live, what to drive and what to say. You are muzzled, much like the ox that treads the corn, and cannot benefit from your labour. You end up being a spectator watching others enjoy what is rightfully yours.

There are many other examples of great men and women that paid the ultimate price for their freedom. Many of them never got to experience the freedom they were willing to lay their lives down for. But to their minds anything was better than the alternative, which was to do nothing and put up with bondage.

There is indeed a suffering associated with obtaining your inheritance in Christ but not in the way that most think. When you are unwell in your body, and you discover in the Word that you are redeemed from sickness and disease, your suffering will be in you doing whatever it takes to confess and believe for your healing until it manifests. That doesn't sound like suffering but if you have ever been unwell you will know it is one of the hardest things to do to stand on a promise of healing when everything in your circumstances is pointing to the contrary. Similarly if you don't have a penny to your name and you know that the Word makes it clear that it is God's will to prosper you and meet your needs, then your suffering will be evidenced in you determining to believe the reality of God's provision in your life until it manifests.

Receive your freedom today in the name of Jesus! Freedom from feelings of guilt and self recrimination. Freedom from negative opinions and all forms of fear and anxiety. Freedom to become the person God created you to be. In this season of your life it is my prayer that you will go free and finally begin to live life on the level that God intended for you. Refuse to take no for an answer.

> *'May grace, (God's favour) and peace (which is perfect well-being, all necessary good, all spiritual prosperity, and freedom from fears and agitating passions and moral conflicts) be multiplied to you in the full, personal, precise, and correct knowledge of God and of Jesus our Lord.' (2 Peter 1:2)*

> *'Let us praise the Lord, the God of Israel, because he has come to help his people and has given them freedom.' (Luke 1:68)*

In political circles, the term 'cost of freedom' means something entirely different. It is usually used as a justification when some overzealous and overpaid civil servant is trying to convince the electorate to give up their civil liberties, submit themselves to intrusive and unwelcome surveillance or pay higher taxes. Secular governments rule their subjects through fear. For many years the threat of Communism was used in different countries around the world to convince their citizens of the need to spend trillions of dollars on armaments necessary to counter this evil. But with the collapse of the USSR and communism, a slew of different other fear inducing events were paraded. Global warming, swine flu and terrorism have all had their time in the limelight. But we remain committed to enforcing our freedom, and that includes freedom from all forms of fear.

I leave you with this quote by Walter Cronkite—*"There is no such thing as a little freedom. Either you are all free, or you are not free."*

Chapter Three

BEWARE THE VAGARIES OF RELIGIOUS THINKING

"Those who deny freedom to others deserve it not for themselves."

Abraham Lincoln

When you read about the great things that Jesus died to give to us, they sound so good that many people struggle to accept them. One of my favourite sayings reads thus: *"God's promises are so extravagant, you have to renew your mind to be able to receive them."*

I spent years hearing messages on renewing the mind, but didn't fully appreciate why this simple process was so important. Fact is, if you don't change the way you think, there are some of God's blessings that will be closed off to you permanently, because your old unregenerate way of thinking simply cannot operate at the higher level God operates on.

> *"For My thoughts are not your thoughts, nor are your ways My ways," says the Lord. "For as the heavens are higher than the earth, so are My ways higher than your ways, and My thoughts than your thoughts." (Isaiah 55:8-9)*

To be able to receive anything from God, we have to get rid of our old fleshly and limited way of thinking and adopt His way of thinking. This was so important to God that when He sent John the Baptist to act as His Son's forerunner, the first words that came out of his mouth had to do with renewing the mind.

> *'In those days there appeared John the Baptist, preaching in the Wilderness of Judea, and saying "Repent, think*

> *differently, change your mind, regretting your sins and changing your conduct, for the kingdom of heaven is at hand.'" (Matthew 3:1-2)*

To be able to usher in this new kingdom, a mindset change was going to be required. A new culture was about to be established, and those who held onto their old culture would be bypassed by the world changing revolution that was brewing.

> *'Thus you have made the commandment of God of no effect by your tradition.' (Matthew 15:6b)*

There is one thing that is more powerful than the Word of God, and that is any tradition that we hold onto that is contrary to the Word, because it will nullify the power that is contained in the Word of God. That's why renewing your mind through the Scriptures is so important.

Tradition is a very powerful thing. I grew up in a denomination that taught unashamedly and with great conviction that poverty brought you closer to God. They even advocated a vow of poverty. I adopted it to a large degree because that was what was on offer, but I never understood how ridiculous it was until I realized that the very denomination that propagated these beliefs was one of the richest institutions in the world. Do as I say and not as I do.

> *'I beseech you therefore brethren, by the mercies of God, that you present your bodies a living sacrifice, holy acceptable to God, which is your reasonable service. And do not be conformed to this world, but be transformed by the renewing of your mind, that you may prove what is that good and acceptable and perfect will of God.' (Romans 12:1-2)*

You can only prove the will of God for your highest good and total freedom when your mind is renewed. If you fail to do that you will forever remain on the outskirts looking in, and wonder for the rest of your life why you aren't making any progress.

Scriptures like, *"Foxes have holes and birds have nests, but the Son of Man has nowhere to lay His head" (Matthew 8:20)* have been used to convince us that Jesus was broke and didn't even have a house, even though this isn't borne out by studying His life. Maybe now is a good time to slaughter this religious cow permanently. The word 'head' in this Scripture is the Greek word *Kephale* and it refers to rule, authority, power and dominion. Foxes use their holes and birds their nests for the purpose of nurturing their young. Understood in context, Jesus was bemoaning the fact that He did not have anyone He could nurture and download His mind into because despite His best efforts, His disciples and others around him were still not the finished article and on many occasions failed to grasp what He was teaching them. They were willing to follow Him but all too often there was a clear disconnect between His level of thinking and theirs.

When Jesus was beginning His ministry, His first public words echoed those uttered by John.

> *'From that time Jesus began to preach, crying out, "Repent, change your mind for the better, heartily amend your ways, with abhorrence of your past sins, for the kingdom of heaven is at hand."' (Matthew 4:17)*

It's going to take a major mindset shift for us to begin to appropriate the many freedoms that are part of the package that God wants to get to us. Somehow there is a tendency to believe that whatever God has laid for us can't be that good and many Christians would sooner believe that God is working against them rather than for them. 2 Corinthians 8:9 is a case in point:

> *"You know the generous grace of our Lord Jesus Christ. Though he was rich, yet for your sakes he became poor, so that by his poverty he could make you rich."*

It is always interesting to watch religious folk try and explain away this scripture, as if somehow it ended up in the Bible by accident. They invariably come up with ways to convince people that God wants them

25

broke, sick, struggling to keep up with their bills, eating substandard food, and in some bizarre way He gets some glory from all of that. Go figure.

Here is another one.

> *'I said, "You are gods, and all of you are children of the Most High."' (Psalm 82:6)*

What a wonderful statement! But how often will well meaning Christians interpret the life out of this scripture, and make you believe that it doesn't mean what it says? Jesus speaking to the Pharisees made an interesting observation:

> *'Then the Jews took up stones again to stone Him. Jesus answered them, "Many good works I have shown you from My Father. For which of those works do you stone Me?" The Jews answered Him, saying, "For a good work we do not stone You, but for blasphemy, and because You, being a Man, make Yourself God."*
>
> *Jesus answered them, "Is it not written in your law,' I said, "You are gods"? If He called them gods, to whom the word of God came (and the Scripture cannot be broken), do you say of Him whom the Father sanctified and sent into the world, 'You are blaspheming,' because I said, 'I am the Son of God'?*

True freedom will come when you start identifying absolutely with who God says you are and do not allow other people's limited opinions to frame your mindset. Your reality will always be framed by what you know. And the natural human tendency is to think that what we know is all there is to know. That's why you have to change your reality by constantly exposing your mind to God's Word and turning it over and over in your mind until you begin to believe what it says about you.

I despise religion. The term religion is derived from the Latin word *'religari'* which means 'to bind'. When you break it down all religion boils down to is a doomed attempt by men to subscribe to God's level of holiness by doing what they perceive to be holy things. So some people will tell you that you can't wear makeup, that if you are a woman you shouldn't wear trousers, and the list goes on and on. None of that brings you any closer to God. If anything it takes you further away because instead of a vibrant, exciting relationship with God, what is left is a convoluted and constantly expanding list of manmade rules and regulations that have no positive power inherent in them, but are just negative and toxic.

> *"These people honour me with their lips, but their hearts are far from me. Their worship is a farce, for they teach man-made ideas as commands from God." (Matthew 15:8-9)*

Jesus' many run-ins with the Pharisees are well chronicled. His main issue with this group stemmed from the fact that, to a casual observer they appeared to be the epitome of spirituality and sincere commitment to God, but in truth they were anything but. They tithed faithfully, fasted twice a week and fastidiously observed the plethora of other laws and regulations laid out by Mosaic Law. However they were more interested in the outward appearance of their works than in any genuine relationship with their Creator. The Jewish historian Josephus even reported that some Pharisees would hire a trumpeter to create as much fanfare as possible when they were about to present their offerings in the temple. Jesus' indictment of them is stirring.

> *'Then Jesus spoke to the multitudes and to His disciples, saying: "The scribes and the Pharisees sit in Moses' seat. Therefore whatever they tell you to observe, that observe and do, but do not do according to their works; for they say, and do not do. For they bind heavy burdens, hard to bear, and lay them on men's shoulders; but they themselves will not move them with one of their fingers. (Matthew 23:1-4)*

> *"But woe to you, scribes and Pharisees, hypocrites! For you shut up the kingdom of heaven against men; for you neither go in yourselves, nor do you allow those who are entering to go in." (v13)*

Possibly the greatest challenge with Christianity is the fact that the very thing that was created by God with the express aim of giving His people genuine freedom is now being used by many to create bondage. Each time you read the Word you can see God's fingerprint through it all, urging the reader to explore the wonderful gifts that are packaged for his or her benefit. But just as in the days of the Pharisees there will always be their modern day equivalent who can't accept the simplicity of the Gospel and the liberties that are freely ours and they elect to reduce our covenant to a lifeless list of rules and regulations.

> *'Now the Lord is the Spirit, and where the Spirit of the Lord is, there is liberty, emancipation from bondage, freedom.' (2 Corinthians 3:17)*

The natural unrenewed mind cannot receive God's forgiveness for sin because the process of getting rid of your sin seems too simplistic.

> *'But if we confess our sins to Him, He is faithful and just to forgive us our sins and to cleanse us from all wickedness.' (1 John 1:9)*

So even after we are born again, we are often racked with feelings of guilt and self-recrimination because our minds continue to condemn us and remind us of how wicked we once were. As a result we do not develop the confidence to take God at His Word, but remain victims to our past.

Religious people will tell you that when you are struggling with a situation, you should just accept it as your lot in life, and not make any attempts to overcome it, because *"that is just your cross to bear"* We must refuse to accept any way of thinking that is diametrically opposed to what the Word of God says.

We are to behave in exactly the same way that Jesus did, demonstrating an unparalleled level of confidence in God and His Word and its ability to transform our lives and the lives of those around us.

> *'Because as He is, so are we in this world.' (1 John 4:17)*

We should beware the very real temptation of using our experiences to invalidate God's Word. Our experiences are only ever valid teaching tools when they confirm what the Word says. It is so easy to go off course when you choose to draw up a doctrine based on your experiences because as pertinent as they are to you, they might not be applicable to someone else's situation. The Word of God is the only legitimate plumb line.

We have even more challenges today with New Age teachings that promise their followers the world, but do not have the ability to deliver because their fundamental premise is flawed. They tell you that you can be successful and that you can achieve this success without a reliance on God, but rather through an unerring focus on the 'supremacy of the human spirit.' These philosophies sound great, but their ultimate sting is that they promise freedom but can only deliver death.

> *"See to it that no one carries you off as spoil or makes you yourselves captive by his so called philosophy and intellectualism and vain deceit, idle fancies and plain nonsense, following human tradition—men's ideas of the material rather than the spiritual world, just crude notions following the rudimentary and elemental teachings of the universe and disregarding the teachings of Christ the Messiah." (Colossians 2:8)*

I probably spent the first six or seven years of my Christian life in a self imposed prison where I was both jailer and prisoner. To my mind, serving God couldn't be something pleasurable, but rather an onerous duty that I had to fulfil for fear of experiencing a fiery end. I prayed, but I didn't actually enjoy it because rather than being an enjoyable conversation with my Daddy, it was a legalistic exercise that left me feeling empty. This mindset affected many of my relationships. I felt it was my job to show people the error of their ways. No wonder many of my friends would politely decline my offers of meeting up. Someone once said that if you live with the judge you will always be on trial. The day I realized what I was doing wrong was a great day, not just for me but for those around me also. Instead of trying to change everyone around me, I had begun to understand the need to simply improve my love walk, and appreciate people regardless of their shortcomings. This simple shift in my philosophy surprisingly resulted in a number of my friends giving their lives to the Lord. I realized that the greatest gift God gave us was His unconditional love, and it was my responsibility to give the same to others.

I also realized that I felt guilty when I was enjoying life, and was sure that I must be doing something wrong.

> *"The thief comes only in order to steal and kill and destroy. I came that they may have and enjoy life, and have it in abundance, to the full, till it overflows."*

We have the right to enjoy our lives, to enjoy our families, enjoy our marriages, rather than get caught up in a mundane lifestyle that destroys our vitality. I get the feeling that a lot of folk will be surprised when they get to heaven because they will realize for the first time that it was part of God's original plan for them to enjoy life and not simply endure it.

Notwithstanding the total freedom we have in Christ, as human beings we continue to manufacture ways of trying to qualify for what has freely been given to us. This is the mindset behind many eastern religions that make you believe that all forms of suffering will entitle you to qualify for God's grace. It is a fallacy that has crippled many of us and yet sadly we seem blind to it.

> *"How foolish can you be! After starting your Christian lives in the Spirit, why are you now trying to become perfect by your own human effort?" (Galatians 3:3)*

So beware of the religious mindset that some well meaning people have adopted. It will destroy your relationships—not just with God, but with those all around you who should be the beneficiaries of your knowledge of God. If you allow them they will leave you restless and discontented, wishing for more. Religion can never satisfy, but a relationship with God can.

> *"They sneaked in to spy on us and take away the freedom we have in Christ Jesus." (Galatians 2:4)*

You have to renew your mind to the reality of God's promises. If you fail to do this you will find yourself stuck in a never ending cycle of defeat and failure. You have to transform your thinking and only then can you begin to experience genuine freedom. The late Norman Vincent Peale put it this way: "*Change your thoughts and you change your world.*"

Run a mile from people who don't expect God to do anything great for them. Flee those folk who have no hope that their lives will change, because if you hang around with them their negativity and lack of expectation will eventually rub off on you and you will quickly find yourself grounded.

> *'Do not be deceived. Bad company corrupts good character.' (1 Corinthians 15:33)*

> *By changing Your thinking,*
> *You change your beliefs;*
> *When you change your beliefs,*
> *You change your expectations;*
> *When you change your expectations,*
> *You change your attitude;*
> *When you change your attitude,*
> *You change your behaviour;*
> *When you change your behaviour,*
> *You change your performance;*
> *When you change your performance;*
> *You Change Your Life!*

> *Author unknown*

Chapter Four

THERE WILL BE GIANTS IN YOUR LAND

"When the war of the giants is over the wars of the pygmies will begin."

Winston Churchill

Every time you make the decision to go to another level in any area of your life, you will encounter opposition. This is an unfortunate fact of life. There will be resistance to your change of level, often by people you do not even know. You will even experience this resistance from spiritual forces that will do whatever they can to keep you grounded and stop you from flying.

> *'For we wrestle not against flesh and blood, but against principalities, against powers, against the rulers of the darkness of this world, against spiritual wickedness in high places.' (Ephesians 6:12)*

There are two possible reactions that you can have when you come up against such opposition. You can either succumb to the pressure, and accept the limitations that are being imposed on you, or you can resist them with everything that you have. It is easier to just give in and settle for what is familiar and comfortable, but it is a lot more rewarding to brave the onslaught against you and press on to greater heights.

So you can't be surprised when things go awry and don't quite work out the way you anticipated. As preachers we are probably guilty of telling people that the moment they get saved everything will be easy and they will never encounter any difficulties, but the reality is very different. I am not an ardent believer in the phrase 'new level, new devil' but there is undoubtedly some truth to it. Even Jesus warned us that we wouldn't always have things our own way.

> *"I have told you these things, so that in Me you may have perfect peace and confidence. In the world you have tribulation and trials and distress and frustration; but be of good cheer, take courage, be confident, certain, undaunted! For I have overcome the world. I have deprived it of power to harm you and have conquered it for you." (John 16:33)*

Life is indeed challenging, and sometimes it can be downright nasty. Those are the vagaries of living in a fallen world. But you cannot afford to let that hold you back. The stories we love to hear and retell are not stories of an easy path to success, but rather tales of overcoming incredible odds, tragedy and adversity to win. We love to talk about David overcoming the giant Goliath, Moses conquering the Red Sea, Elijah overcoming 850 prophets of Baal and Ashtoreth. These are the stories that stir us up and motivate us to do greater things in our own lives.

> *"The greater the obstacle, the more glory in overcoming it."*
> *(Moliere)*

You must develop the confidence to see yourself as significant to God's plan in the earth, and to realize that regardless of how big the obstacles may be that you face, you are well able to fulfil your assignment. That is the essence of true freedom—to accomplish the purpose for which you were put on the earth.

My story is no different to yours. I have crammed a lot of overcoming into the years I have been on the earth. Some of the areas that we overcome may not win you any public awards, but they are no less significant. I have battled to stay married to the wife of my youth despite a less than perfect start to our union. We have had to endure the mocking of those who never thought we would make it because we got married young and had a child out of wedlock. We have had to deal with the loss of loved ones at critical times in our lives. We have had to overcome being vilified for standing up for the truth, when it would have been easier to simply go with the flow. And there have been times when we have been tempted to give up. But each time the strength that God gave us kept us fighting for our next level.

Our first son spent the first two years of his life wearing hand me downs because we couldn't clothe him any other way. We sold everything from sweets to peanuts just to make sure we could feed him and ourselves. We had to endure the sneers and smirks of those who thought we would never make it. But deep down we knew that we were created for a much better life and we fought tooth and nail to make it a reality.

I am urging you not to lose your passion and vitality just because things haven't worked out the way you anticipated. Don't be deceived into believing that whatever God has prepared for you will simply fall into your lap without any effort on your part. Nothing could be further from the truth. All too often, even after God has pointed out your inheritance to you, He still expects you to play your part. That part may often require displaying a level of doggedness that is alien to those who are unwilling to fight for the things that belong to them.

> *'After forty days of exploring the land, the men returned to the camp. They came back to Moses and Aaron and all the Israelites at Kadesh, in the Desert of Paran. The men reported to them and showed everybody the fruit from the land. They told Moses, "We went to the land where you sent us, and it is a fertile land! Here is some of its fruit. But the people who live there are strong. Their cities are walled and very large. We even saw some Anakites there . . ."*
>
> *Then Caleb told the people near Moses to be quiet, and he said, "We should certainly go up and take the land for ourselves. We can certainly do it." But the men who had gone with him said, "We can't attack those people; they are stronger than we are." And those men gave the Israelites a bad report about the land they explored, saying, "The land that we explored is too large to conquer. All the people we saw are very*

> *tall. We saw the Nephilim people there. We felt like grasshoppers, and we looked like grasshoppers to them."*
> *(Numbers 13:25-33)*

God knew that there were giants in the land before He told them to go in to possess it. In fact it was part of His strategy to empower the children of Israel to eliminate the Nephilim, a mutant race that were the product of an evil union between the fallen angels and human beings. In God's eyes the battle was already won, if only they would show up for the fight. Then He would demonstrate His power and back them all the way. When we line up with God's agenda, we become irresistible, because nothing can stand in the way of His purposes.

> *'Declaring the end from the beginning, and from ancient times things that are not yet done, saying, "My counsel shall stand, and I will do all My pleasure . . . indeed I have spoken it; I will also bring it to pass. I have purposed it; I will also do it"' (Isaiah 46:10-11)*

Nothing frustrates God more than a lack of faith and a lack of confidence in His promises. If you are unwilling to confront your enemies you will never conquer them. Only when you are immoveable in the face of opposition will you experience true freedom. There are forces at play whose sole purpose is to enslave you at every opportunity.

> *"And from the days of John the Baptist until now the kingdom of heaven suffers violence, and the violent take it by force." (Matthew 11:12)*

Whenever you take strides to reach out and fulfil your destiny, expect opposition, ridicule and contempt. They are par for the course. Lester Sumrall often told the story of how his own father tried to dissuade him from heeding God's call to preach, telling him that he would starve to death. Another close relative told him he wouldn't make it in a thousand years. But we all know how his life and ministry turned out. What a great gift to the body of Christ!

When Nehemiah returned to rebuild the walls of Jerusalem, a divine mandate began its fulfilment. On cue, enter Sanballat and Tobiah, his most ardent critics.

> *'But it so happened, when Sanballat heard that we were rebuilding the wall, that he was furious and very indignant, and mocked the Jews. And he spoke before his brethren and the army of Samaria, and said, "What are these feeble Jews doing? Will they fortify themselves? Will they offer sacrifices? Will they complete it in a day? Will they revive the stones from the heaps of rubbish—stones that are burned?" Now Tobiah the Ammonite was beside him, and he said, "Whatever they build, if even a fox goes up on it, he will break down their stone wall."' (Nehemiah 4:1-2)*

Nehemiah however was undeterred, and determined to fulfil his assignment, he oversaw the building programme with his men, holding a building tool in one hand and a sword in the other. Whatever the size of your opposition, your level of persistence must follow suit.

When the resistance comes against you, the first tool that will be used against you is to cast doubt on your ability and competence to fulfil your assignment. When we first started pastoring, we had one couple in particular who made it their business to question whether we were able to do the job because we were much younger than them! Someone needed to gently remind them that many of the people God chose for great works were very young also, and many were teenagers. David, Mary, Samuel and Jeremiah are just a few examples that spring to mind.

Then if that doesn't seem to work, your critics will even cast doubt on your motives for doing what you are doing. They will accuse you of being self seeking, driven by ambition and not a genuine desire to help others. Sanballat and Tobiah openly accused Nehemiah of the same things, calling into question his reasons for rebuilding the walls and implying that it was for selfish reasons. Don't be intimidated. The majority very rarely initiate anything of value. On occasion they may confirm it, but it will still be necessary for you to have a dogged determination to build something of value, regardless of the accusations that are being thrown at you. The day may come when they are forced to admit that they were wrong, but even if that day never comes, you will still have the satisfaction of knowing that you are on your way to fulfilling destiny.

> *"Great spirits have always found violent opposition from mediocrities. The latter cannot understand it when a man does not thoughtlessly submit to hereditary prejudices but honestly and courageously uses his intelligence." Albert Einstein*

Then if those tactics still don't work, your adversaries will try and use fear to intimidate you into giving up on your assignment.

> *'But Sanballat, Tobiah, the Arabs, the Ammonites, and the people from Ashdod were very angry when they heard that the repairs to Jerusalem's walls were continuing and that the holes in the wall were being closed. So they all made plans to come to Jerusalem and fight and stir up trouble. But we prayed to our God and appointed guards to watch for them day and night. (Nehemiah 4:7-9)*

Fear is paralyzing. Don't for a moment entertain fear, because it will cripple you mentally and physically. Once you begin to fear, your capacity to be enterprising and innovative is dulled, and you join the ranks of those who refuse to attempt anything out of the ordinary because they are afraid of what may happen.

> *'The Lord is on my side; I will not fear. What can man do to me? The Lord is for me among those who help me; Therefore I shall see my desire on those who hate me.' (Psalm 118:6-7)*

Do not pursue peace at any cost if it means giving up on something that is contained in your covenant package. It is a truism of modern day politicking that one should never negotiate with terrorists. That is what is wrong with pacifism, a movement that pursues a peaceful solution to conflict at any cost. There will be many seasons where we have to fight because God demands it.

> *"They have also healed the hurt of My people slightly,*
> *Saying, 'Peace, peace!' when there is no peace."*
> *(Jeremiah 6:14)*

The worst thing you can do is refuse to fight when a fight is the only way out of your predicament. Many a destiny has been aborted because the people involved did not have the heart to bite the bullet and make the tough decisions that were necessary.

> *'And cursed is he who keeps his sword back from blood.'*
> *(Jeremiah 48:10b)*

Jesus was aware of the need for conflict in carrying out His purpose. Just because everyone is not falling over themselves to fall in line with your established objective does not mean that you are wrong.

> *"Do not think that I came to bring peace on earth. I*
> *did not come to bring peace but a sword. For I have*
> *come to 'set a man against his father, a daughter*
> *against her mother, and a daughter-in-law against*
> *her mother-in-law'; and 'a man's enemies will be those*
> *of his own household." (Matthew 10:34-36)*

Ferdinand Marcos, the former President of the Philippines made a much quoted statement. He said, "*We cannot and we will not negotiate with terrorists. We have nothing but contempt for them . . .*" In the 2010 film "*Unthinkable*" in a particularly riveting scene, someone mentions to Samuel L. Jackson, that the United States did not negotiate with terrorists to which Jackson retorted, "*We do it all the time.*"

Terrorists don't come much bigger than the devil and his cronies. When you really look at it they are behind every form of bondage known to man, using as they do human vehicles. The devil will do whatever he can to keep you in bondage and even when you are on your way to freedom, he will still try and keep something of a hold on you. It's a bit like having an ex-girlfriend who regardless of the fact that you are no longer in a relationship with her still tries to enforce her rights to you. Think of the character of Alex Forrest as played by Glenn Close in the 80's movie *Fatal Attraction*. The mindset is 'if I can't have you then no one can.' Even when you force the devil into a corner and demand that he releases you, he will still try and negotiate with you.

> *"I will let you go, that ye may sacrifice to the Lord your God in the wilderness, only you shall not go far away" (Exodus 8:28)*

In Israel's case, Pharaoh was still trying to act as if he was in the driving seat, even though God had shown unequivocally just who was in charge. Just like Moses couldn't trust Pharaoh's word, neither can you trust the devil when he promises to let you go.

> *"He was a murderer from the beginning, not holding to the truth, for there is no truth in him. When he lies, he speaks his native language, for he is a liar and the father of lies." (John 8:44)*

The Old Testament is full of stories of people who refused to back down when threats were made to their freedom. Shadrech, Mishech and Abednego chose the fate of the furnace rather than accept a freedom that was really no freedom at all. Daniel chose the fate of entering the lions den rather than have someone else encroach on his right to worship God. These stories are particularly relevant when you consider all of the moves, using legislation, fear or accusations that are being implemented all over the world to encroach upon the rights of Christians to worship in freedom.

Our path to complete freedom will always be littered with critics and detractors. William Wilberforce, the great advocate of equality for all men regardless of their colour, fought a difficult and lonely battle against an entire political and economic system that was benefiting from the evil system of slavery. He had an abundance of enemies but this did not hinder his resolve to fulfil his assignment.

"So enormous, so dreadful, so irremediable did the Trade's wickedness appear that my own mind was completely made up for Abolition. Let the consequences be what they would, I from this time determined that I would never rest until I had effected its abolition."

He also said:

"Can you tell a plain man the road to heaven? Certainly, turn at once to the right, then go straight forward."

Do you want to know the way to experience days of heaven on earth? Go straight forward! Just as God told Moses, when he was confronted by the Red Sea, "Move Forward", we should adopt that as our slogan. Move Forward! Move Forward! Move Forward!

Even when things don't work out the way you had planned, don't give up! I learnt that lesson a long time ago. There were a number of businesses I tried that for one reason or another never seemed to work out, and it was always difficult to haul yourself back up again and give it another go, but each time we did, and each time we got stronger and stronger and the results got better and better. Don't listen to the people who specialise in not making mistakes, and as a result end up doing nothing of significance. Someone once said, "I would rather wear out than rust out."

"It behooves every man to remember that the work of the critic is of altogether secondary importance, and that in the end, progress is accomplished by the man who does things." Theodore Roosevelt

To experience freedom you will have to contend with a group of people who will make it their purpose in life to criticize your every move and ridicule every step of your upward progression. There is nothing you can do to stop this bunch of piranhas from congregating. To try and counter them would be a full time job. Your responsibility is to ensure that you don't allow other people's opinions to stop you from enjoying every one of the liberties that are rightfully yours.

God is well aware that we will always have folk around us who are not best pleased at our progress. But He has a simple solution. He promises to give us the victory in the midst of the opposition.

> *'Yea, though I walk through the valley of the shadow of death, I will fear no evil, for You are with me. Your rod and Your staff they comfort me. You prepare a table before me in the presence of my enemies.' (Psalm 23:4-5)*

That's why it is so unfortunate when we allow other people's perceptions of us to stop us dead in our tracks. The fear of what people will think of us can be such a hindering factor.

> *"Far better it is to dare mighty things, to win glorious triumphs even though checkered by failure, than to rank with those poor spirits who neither enjoy nor suffer much because they live in the gray twilight that knows neither victory nor defeat." Theodore Roosevelt*

There will be seasons where you will feel discouraged and ready to throw in the towel but always remind yourself that you can only lose when you decide that you don't want to fight anymore.

Anytime you try to bring glory to God, you will experience opposition. And the way you bring glory to God is by becoming the very best that you can become. Remember, *"God's glory is man fully alive."* God is never more excited that when He sees you firing on all cylinders, passionate about life, and well on your way to fulfilling your purpose.

I am a huge boxing fan and one of my favourite things in the time leading up to the actual fight is the stare down between the two fighters. That is often the moment when the fight is either won or lost. When the fighters look deep into each other's eyes and see fear and uncertainty, they automatically know that they have the edge. But it is even more riveting when you see the fighters talking smack to one another. The whole idea is to scare the other fighter into believing that your insults and threats will become their reality. Much like Goliath did when speaking to Saul and his armies.

> *'And the Philistine said, "I defy the armies of Israel this day; give me a man that we may fight together."' When Saul and all Israel heard these words of the Philistine, they were dismayed and greatly afraid. (1 Samuel 17:10-11)*

Goliath then tried the same thing with David.

> *'And when the Philistine looked about him and saw David, he disdained him for he was only a youth, ruddy and good looking . . . And the Philistine cursed David by his gods. And the Philistine said to David, "Come to me, and I will give your flesh to the birds of the air and the beasts of the field!"' (v42-44)*

But David was all too aware that the greatest weapon to use when fear is trying to overwhelm you is a mouth that invokes the full force of God's promises.

> *'Then David said to the Philistine, "You come to me with a sword, with a spear and with a javelin. But I come to you in the name of the Lord of Hosts, the God of the armies of Israel, whom you have defied. This day the Lord will deliver you into my hand and I will strike you and take your head from you. And this day I will give the carcasses of the camp of the Philistines to the birds of the air and the wild beasts of the earth, that all the earth may know that there is a God in Israel."' (v45-46)*

God has given us such a marvellous gift, which when used properly will snatch victory out of the clutches of defeat. I use the term 'extravagant declarations' to describe the kinds of words that must come out of our mouths. Speak boldly and consistently, and God will back you every step of the way.

But possibly the greatest tool that the devil will use is the force of discouragement.

> *'Then Judah said, "The strength of the labourers is failing, and there is so much rubbish that we are not able to build the wall." (Nehemiah 4:10)*

Discouragement is so deadly because it is the inevitable result when fear and doubt have set in, and you now begin to abort your destiny with your own mouth. Immediately after the incredible victory that Elijah experienced at Mt Carmel over the prophets of Baal, it took just a few words of mean intent from Jezebel to turn him into a quivering mess.

> *'Then Jezebel sent a messenger to Elijah saying, "So let the gods do to me, and more also, if I do not make your life as the life of one of them by tomorrow about this time."' And when he saw that, he ran for his life, and went to Beersheba . . . and came and sat down under a broom tree. And he prayed that he might die, and said, "It is enough! Now Lord take my life for I am no better than my fathers."'(1 Kings 19:1-4)*

Discouragement can often set in after some of your greatest victories, but it is always designed to stop you from reaching even greater heights. And the main reason it works is because you start to believe that you are all on your own and that nobody can help you out of your predicament.

> *"I alone am left and they seek to take my life." (v14)*

God quickly pointed out to Elijah that He had seven thousand other followers in Israel who were committed to His cause. And we must be encouraged by this too. God is too wise to ever run out of options.

Discouragement will steal your vision, and rob you of your strength and confidence. Do not allow it to set in. God is always on your side and with Him on your side, victory is guaranteed!

> *'And when the servant of the man of God arose early
> and went out, there was an army, surrounding the
> city with horses and chariots. And his servant said
> to him, "Alas, my master! What shall we do?" So he
> answered, Do not fear, for those who are with us are
> more than those who are with them." And Elisha
> prayed and said, "Lord, I pray, open his eyes that he
> may see." Then the Lord opened the eyes of the young
> man and he saw. And behold, the mountain was full
> of horses and chariots of fire all around Elisha." (2
> Kings 6:15-17)*

Do not allow anything to stop you from achieving the great destiny that lies unfulfilled in your bosom. Do not give in to the subtle lure of the enemy to live a life of ignominy and insignificance. I refuse to be a footnote in the annals of history! You and I were created to be headliners!

If you are unwilling to do it for yourself, then do it for your mother, who never experienced abundance in her life because she was always working hard to give the very best to you. Do it for your wife who has stood beside you through all the lean years and the many ups and downs. Do it for your children so that they don't have to start out scraping the bottom of the barrel like you did. Do it for those who will come after you so that they may be inspired by a life that was of generational significance.

> *"Fight for your brothers, your sons, your daughters,
> your wives and your houses". (Nehemiah 4:14)*

Make the decision today to be the last man standing, regardless of the opposition that lies before you. Your inheritance is waiting for you. Reach for it!

Chapter Five

DARE TO DREAM

"You see things; and you say, 'Why?' But I dream things that never were; and I say, 'Why not?'"

George Bernard Shaw

In 2009, a 47 year old Susan Boyle shocked the world with her rendition of *Les Miserables* "*I dreamed a Dream*", on the hugely popular English show *Britain's Got Talent*. It catapulted her into instant fame and stardom. Her audition was viewed over 100 million times on YouTube over the next 9 days. In the course of the next few weeks she made appearances on the *Oprah Winfrey Show* and *Larry King Live*. Her first album went on to sell 9 million copies in six weeks and this earned her recognition by the Guinness Book of Records for a string of records including being the oldest person in the UK to reach number one with a debut album. It really was the perfect definition of a rags to riches story.

What is so intriguing about her story is that one of the first questions that Simon Cowell, one of the judges asked Susan when she came on stage was "What's the dream," to which she replied, "I am trying to be a professional singer." In many of the available recordings of her audition, a young girl can be seen sneering at her answer. I am pretty sure she wishes she hadn't done that now, because she stands out today as an unfortunate poster girl for critics all over the world, who are standing by waiting to mock whatever dream you have. Whenever you make the decision to pursue your dream, you can be sure that there will be many who will make it their business to mock and ridicule you. But do not let this stop you from dreaming.

One of the lines in "*I dreamed a dream*" reads, "*I had a dream my life would be so different from the hell I'm living, so different now from what it seemed, now life has killed the dream I dreamed.*"

Every one of us has a God given dream. We are all born with a dream resident in our bosoms which we are meant to accomplish in our lifetime. But for many different reasons, many of those dreams die before they are ever fulfilled. Life in its own inimitable way has the ability to destroy dreams, crush hope and destroy passion.

In the Bedfordshire village in which we used to live, there was an old man well into his sixties who cleaned the streets of the village. The very first time I saw him, it was almost as if God afforded me a window into his soul. I saw a man who had come to England from the Caribbean with great dreams and aspirations, much like Dick Whittington, expecting to see the streets paved with gold. But year after year, and decade after decade of unfulfilled expectations produced a man whose dream had died, and someone who had accepted his lot in life, accepting that he was destined to live a life of mediocrity and insignificance.

To dream means to imagine as possible what God has called you to do. It means to allow your mind to soar beyond the limits of temporary pain and discomfort and see yourself becoming the great person you were destined to become.

On the 28th of August 1963, on the steps of the Lincoln Memorial in Washington DC, Martin Luther King Jnr. delivered one of his greatest speeches, calling for racial equality and an end to discrimination.—*I have a dream.* Here is an excerpt from that famous speech:

> "*I say to you today, my friends, that in spite of the difficulties and frustrations of the moment, I still have a dream. It is a dream deeply rooted in the American dream.*
>
> *I have a dream that one day this nation will rise up and live out the true meaning of its creed: "We hold*

these truths to be self-evident: that all men are created equal."

I have a dream that one day on the red hills of Georgia the sons of former slaves and the sons of former slave owners will be able to sit down together at a table of brotherhood.

I have a dream that one day even the state of Mississippi, a desert state, sweltering with the heat of injustice and oppression, will be transformed into an oasis of freedom and justice.

I have a dream that my four children will one day live in a nation where they will not be judged by the color of their skin but by the content of their character.

I have a dream today.

I have a dream that one day every valley shall be exalted, every hill and mountain shall be made low, the rough places will be made plain, and the crooked places will be made straight, and the glory of the Lord shall be revealed, and all flesh shall see it together.

When we let freedom ring, when we let it ring from every village and every hamlet, from every state and every city, we will be able to speed up that day when all of God's children, black men and white men, Jews and Gentiles, Protestants and Catholics, will be able to join hands and sing in the words of the old Negro spiritual, "Free at last! free at last! thank God Almighty, we are free at last!"

He never lived to see the fulfilment of his dream, but millions of people today enjoy the liberties that he saw in his dream nearly 50 years ago.

Nelson Mandela had a dream of seeing a free South Africa, free from the unfortunate excesses of Apartheid. Mahatma Gandhi had a dream of the nation of India delivered from the ravages of British cruelty and oppression. Lester Sumrall dreamed of spreading the message of God's love and mercy to all nations in the world, and eventually reached over 90% of the world's population. I ask you today what is your dream?

If you let it, life will present you with your own serving of shattered hopes and dreams. Your failures, your weaknesses and your shortcomings will conspire to convince you that there is no hope for you and that you are doomed to a life of defeat and despair.

But in the book of Joel, God gives a wonderful promise.

> *"And it shall come to pass afterward, that I will pour out my spirit upon all flesh and your sons and your daughters shall prophesy; your old men shall dream dreams, your young men shall see visions."* God says you will dream again, because His Holy Spirit has awakened every dream that has died in your life! CS Lewis put it this way—*"You are never too old to set another goal or to dream a new dream."*

I want to introduce you to a world of possibility where all of your God given dreams can come true. Don't listen to the naysayers and the haters who try and convince you that you cannot become great, or that things are impossible. They try and tell you to keep it real, and tell the truth. But Douglas H Everett said, *"There are some people who live in a dream world and there are some who face reality; and then there are those who turn one into the other."*

Joseph was just seventeen when he had his dream. He was a teenager who God gave a dream that would result in the deliverance of the whole world from starvation and destruction. In typical fashion, his brothers mocked him for his dream, mostly we can presume because he was so young.

> *'Then Joseph had a dream, and when he told it to his brothers, they hated him even more. Then his brothers*

> *said to him, "Are you actually going to reign over us? Or are you really going to rule over us?" So they hated him even more for his dreams and for his words."*
> *(Genesis 37:5,8)*

This is a clarion call to all people, young and old, to cherish their dreams and not to give up on them regardless of who does or doesn't believe in them. Please deliver me from a generation of young people who want to spend their best years and strength serving the devil, and then belatedly give the Lord what is left. The dream you have is God given. He is speaking to you, as He did to the prophet Jeremiah and encouraging you not to give up in the face of what you perceive to be the many reasons why you can't succeed.

> *'But the Lord said to me, "Do not say, I am a youth, because everywhere I send you, you shall go, and all that I command you, you shall speak. Do not be afraid of them, for I am with you to deliver you," declares the Lord.' (Jeremiah 1:7-8)*

It is interesting to note that Joseph's brothers hated him already. His dream only served to reinforce that hatred. His father Jacob's obvious love for him is what made them hate him, and things only got worse when he made a special coat for his son. Someone once said, "*Favour aint fair.*" Now is the time to stop apologising for and trying to explain away what God is doing in your life, and just enjoy it.

Do remember also that some of the people who will oppose your dream most vociferously are the very ones who will benefit the most from it. If you allow their hatred and opposition to discourage you and stunt your progress, they will suffer the consequences. Imagine what would have happened if Joseph hadn't gone on to be premier of Egypt and institute a brilliant economic programme that guaranteed food supplies for the entire world. His brothers and their families would have died!

It would have been more prudent for his brothers, instead of being jealous and intimidated by his dream to ask to get in on the act. I certainly would have, and asked him for a position in his new cabinet! But instead, Joseph's brothers tried to abort his vision and in doing so actually helped him to accomplish it. Much like the Pharisees tried to abort Jesus' vision and instead helped to accomplish it by crucifying him. The lesson in that for all of us is to allow the negativity we will endure as we go towards our dream to be the propeller that drives us ever closer to its fulfilment.

I have always wondered why God would give you a glimpse of what you were going to become and then allow you to experience all kinds of trauma immediately afterwards. But the answer is really quite obvious. Knowing what He has said about where you are destined, gives you the ability to persevere because it enables you to see beyond the temporary discomfort and difficulty that you may be experiencing. Much like Jesus, who is our example in all things did.

> *'Fixing our eyes on Jesus, the author and perfecter of our faith, who for the joy set before Him endured the cross, despising the shame and has sat down at the right hand of the throne of God. For consider Him who has endured such hostility by sinners against Himself, so that you will not grow weary and lose heart.' (Hebrews 12:2-3)*

A few years ago, in a meeting in Canada, Bishop Tudor Bismark gave me a prophetic word warning me that I was about to enter a time of stretching, emotionally, spiritually and financially, but that the Lord was with me, and would see me through it. At the time things were going along swimmingly, but literally a week after I received that Word, things just fell apart all around me. And the one thing that kept us going and gave us great comfort was that the Lord had in His own inimitable way warned us of what lay ahead. We knew that His promises were as good as money in the bank and that if we held onto them, we would indeed see the end of our faith.

> *'Declaring the end from the beginning, and from ancient times the things not yet done, saying, "My counsel shall stand, and I will do all my pleasure. Calling a ravenous bird from the East, and the man who executes my purpose from a far country. Truly,*

I have spoken, truly I will bring it to pass. I have planned it, surely I will do it.'" (Isaiah 46:10-11)

I don't know what has happened in your life that has caused you to give up on your dreams. Maybe you were taught not to dream, and to manage your expectations, because *"good things don't happen to people like you."* Or maybe you have dreamt for so long and nothing happened that you just feel like it will never happen. Maybe you have suspended your dreams because you feel like they are just costing you too much and you have gone back to the 'comfort' of the mundane and familiar. Whatever the reason may be, I am encouraging you today to dream again! The Bible tells us it is better to be a living dog than a dead lion. As long as you are still alive, you can win, as long as you don't give up.

Habakkuk 2:3 "For the vision is yet for an appointed time, but at the end it shall speak, and not lie: though it tarry, wait for it; because it will surely come, it will not tarry."

And finally, I am encouraging you not to just dream again, but to enlarge the size of your dream. If you were to accomplish your dream in its present form, would it change other people's lives? Does it have the capacity to transform your community, or your nation, or will it just impact positively on your life? Dream big! There are no prizes for small dreams. Dream as if you couldn't fail and watch God back you every step of the way.

"To dream anything that you want to dream. That's the beauty of the human mind. To do anything that you want to do. That is the strength of the human will. To trust yourself to test your limits. That is the courage to succeed." Bernard Edmonds

Chapter Six

STUDY YOUR COVENANT!

"I think we must get rid of slavery or we must get rid of freedom."

Ralph Waldo Emerson

Read Your Bible, Pray Every Day

Read your Bible, pray every day,
Pray every day, pray every day,
Read your Bible, pray every day,
And you'll grow, grow, grow.
And you'll grow, grow, grow.
And you'll grow, grow, grow.
Read your Bible, pray every day,
And you'll grow, grow, grow.

Neglect your Bible, forget to pray,
Forget to pray, forget to pray,
Neglect your Bible, forget to pray,
And you'll shrink, shrink, shrink.
And you'll shrink, shrink, shrink.
And you'll shrink, shrink, shrink.
Neglect your Bible, forget to pray,
And you'll shrink, shrink, shrink.

Author Unknown

The Latin phrase *caveat subscriptor* warns you of your responsibility to ensure that whenever you are about to sign your name to an agreement, that you have read and understood all of the terms contained in it, including the fine print. How many of us can identify with having signed a contract and then realized much later that its conditions were more onerous that we initially thought and yet we were now committed? This has happened thousands of times to folk buying houses or cars, getting married, or starting a new job. Amazingly the lesson is never learnt and we continue to see people falling into the same traps with ever more dire consequences.

Another important legal maxim is '*ignorantia juris non excusat*' translated 'ignorance of the law is no excuse'. Pleading ignorance of the existence of a speed limit on a stretch of road, or insisting that you were not aware that you couldn't park in a certain bay does not exempt you from the consequences when they come.

It is often said that 'ignorance is bliss.' In the 90's the female RnB group SWV sang a song called 'You're the One'. Verse one read:

> *I know that you're somebody else's guy*
> *But these feelings that I have for you I can't deny*
> *She doesn't treat you*
> *The way you want her to*
> *So come on stop fronting*
> *I wanna get with you*
> *What you'r girl don't know won't hurt her*
> *(Hurt her)*
> *Anything to make this love go further*

The song, which is about a young lady trying to convince a man she is interested in to have a relationship with her behind his girlfriend/wife's back highlights the commonly held belief that the things we don't know don't hurt us. She figures if the other woman doesn't know about the illicit relationship, then she can't be hurt. But nothing could be further from the truth. It is often the things we don't know that cause us the greatest harm.

We have a similar scenario developing today where so many of us have signed up to the salvation package given to us freely by God, but we have stubbornly refused to read the terms or the fine print of that package—as a result we suffer the same difficulties and challenges as those who don't even have the rights that we have. We then look increasingly foolish as the years go by with no tangible results to speak of, despite the fact that we are heirs to a marvellous inheritance.

> *'He said to them, "To you it has been given to know the mysteries of the kingdom of God, but to the rest it is in parables, so that seeing they may not see, and hearing they may not understand."' (Luke 8:10)*

Which one of us waits until August to open our Christmas presents? That would be absurd wouldn't it? If you were excited about the gifts you were expecting, you would be champing at the bit to open them on Christmas Eve and even before that, especially if you could see them sitting there invitingly under your tree. Yet we have Bibles that we bought that we have never read, and great commentaries on the Word that still lie untouched. Consequently we remain strangers to our covenant privileges. When this happens you will unwittingly put up with bondage when by right you should be free.

> *'Remember that you were at that time separated, living apart from Christ, excluded from all part in Him, utterly estranged and outlawed from the rights of Israel as a nation, and strangers with no share in the sacred compacts of the Messianic promise, with no knowledge of or right in God's agreements, His covenants. And you had no hope, no promise; you were in the world without God.' (Ephesians 2:12)*

The whole basis of our relationship with God is an understanding of covenant. A covenant is a solemn agreement entered into by two or more parties to carry out the terms they have agreed on. God has entered into a covenant with us. Under this covenant we have certain obligations to fulfil, but the same covenant also confers on us a huge number of amazing benefits. These include salvation, healing, protection, peace, restoration and wealth.

However, no matter how great God's promises are, the onus is still on you to search them out. You have to be willing to pay the price through diligent study, otherwise you will see others who have made the effort walking in the reality of those same promises and you will not be any nearer to appropriating them for yourself.

God has hidden in His Word some glorious revelations of the true extent of our inheritance, and so if you skim read the Word you will never discover them. Gold is rarely found on the surface!

> *'It is the glory of God to conceal a thing: but the honour of kings is to search out a matter.' (Proverbs 25:2)*

A great example of this is the blessings that belong to us under the Abrahamic covenant.

> *'For the promise that he would be the heir of the world was not to Abraham or to his seed through the law, but through the righteousness of faith.' (Romans 4:13)*

Heir of the world! What a wonderful promise! God has given us dominion that isn't just limited to the town or city you live in, but extends to the entire world. Your business should not be limited to your city only, but the whole world should become your clientele. Your influence should not be felt in one little corner of the world, but should span all seven continents of the earth.

So much freedom should flow to you from this one promise. There may be all kinds of restrictions on you right now because you might not have the relevant visas to be living where you are. But when you change your perspective and begin to realize that the entire world is your inheritance, you begin to realize that no man made borders can hem you in. If you can't travel right now, start an internet based business. Get other people to travel on your behalf until you are in a position to travel yourself. Let your mind soar and allow yourself to see the entire planet as your playing field. Buy a map and speak to your territory, instead of allowing the borders that you can't even see to hinder you.

When you embark on an adventure in the Word, you open up new worlds of possibility for yourself. But if you refuse to exercise diligence in this area you will find yourself stuck in a never ending cycle of doubt and self imposed limitations.

Most countries in the world have a constitution that guarantees certain rights to its citizens. Many organizations have a mission statement that outlines its vision as well as its commitment to the well-being of those tasked with bringing the vision to reality. Gangs, whether organized crime outfits such as the Mafia or more localized outfits such as the Bloods or Crips each have an unwritten set of rules that they are all intimately acquainted with that tell them the privileges they can enjoy as members of that gang.

Yet it remains one of the greatest mysteries why so many Christians refuse to acquaint themselves with the intricacies of their governing document. Statistical research shows that less than 10% of professing Christians have read the entire Bible. An individual of average reading ability can read the Bible in 90 hours. That works out to one hour a day for three months or 15 minutes a day for a year.

It seems like a small thing, but it really is a big deal. All too often the things that stop us from enjoying the full extent of our freedoms are the simple things. Slothfulness and tardiness in reading the Book that guarantees our rights, and an unwillingness to renew our minds by meditating on the incredible truths contained in the Word, all contribute to the status quo of a severely limited life.

> *'This Book of the Law shall not depart from your mouth, but you shall meditate in it day and night, that you may observe to do according to all that is written in it. For then you will make your way prosperous, and then you will have good success.' (Joshua 1:8)*

If you want to be free from the bondage that ensnares so many people, you have to be committed to investigating the simple yet effective ways in which you can begin to protect yourselves from falling into bondage.

'How can a young man keep his way pure? By guarding it according to thy word. With my whole heart I seek thee; let me not wander from thy commandments. I have laid up thy word in my heart,—that I might not sin against thee.' (Psalm 119:9-11)

Mark Twain once said, "*People say when they get to heaven, they'll fly around from cloud to cloud playing a harp; but I don't see too many people trying to learn how to fly or too many taking harp lessons to get ready for the event.*"

We say we want to enjoy all that God has to offer us, but how many of us even know what is on offer? Eventually we resort to getting other people to read the Book for us and then tell us what it says. That might have been necessary in times gone by when most people couldn't read, but what it our excuse today?

Many famous people believed that the Bible was a vital tool for life. Abraham Lincoln said, "*I believe the Bible is the best gift God has ever given to man. All the good from the Saviour of the world is communicated to us through this book.*"

In 1839 Alexander Campbell wrote, "*The Bible is to the intellectual and moral world of man what the sun is to the planets in our system,—the fountain and source of light and life, spiritual and eternal . . . The Bible, or the Old and New Testaments, in Hebrew and Greek, contains a full and perfect revelation of God and his will, adapted to man as he now is. It speaks of man as he was, and also as he will hereafter be: but it dwells on man as he is, and as he ought to be . . .*"

You can never rise higher than the quality of the ideas you are exposed to. The Bible reveals to us the mind of God, and there is no better way to know who we should be than seeing our lives through the eyes of God and His original plan for our lives.

'Study to show yourself approved to God, a workman that needs not to be ashamed, rightly dividing the word of truth.' (2 Timothy 2:15)

When you refuse to study, you set yourself up to be ashamed and embarrassed. There are so many rights and privileges contained in your covenant that you will simply never know if all you do is cast a cursory glance over its contents. You will allow mean men to laud it over you and glumly accept a standard of living that is far below what you are entitled to. As my dad used to say to me so many times during my school years, "*Study, study, study.*"

William Shakespeare once said, "*There is no darkness but ignorance.*" The only thing one needs to do to eliminate the darkness is turn on the light. The Word is the only light you need to eliminate every form of darkness in your life. Activate its power in your life and watch it transform your life.

> '*The entrance of Your words gives light; it gives understanding to the simple.*' *(Psalm 119:130)*

Our greatest errors in life will more often than not stem from an abject ignorance of who and what we really are. We give up our liberties and subject ourselves to tyranny when we aren't diligent in establishing definitively what the power of God has already accomplished on our behalf.

> "*You are in error, through ignorance of the Scriptures and of the power of God.*" *(Matthew 22:29)*

Our assignment therefore must be to re-educate ourselves and others. Not in a random way, but through a systematic process of teaching that will finally ring the death knell on all forms of spiritual captivity. Benjamin Franklin rightly said, "*A nation of well informed men who have been taught to know and prize the rights which God has given them cannot be enslaved. It is in the region of ignorance that tyranny begins.*"

It will surprise us to discover that so many of the traditions we hold as dear and sacred have absolutely no basis in the Word of God. Unless you are fortunate and discover this truth early on, it may be too late to do anything about it when you do eventually find out.

I grew up believing in a God who was sadistically waiting to pounce on every single mistake I made, and this mindset severely hindered the vitality of my relationship with Him. I also thought that God wanted me to be poor, because I thought that poverty was synonymous with holiness. I don't think that way anymore because I read the Book and discovered a God of incredible love and mercy who is committed to my highest good.

> *'O give thanks unto the Lord; for he is good: for his mercy endureth for ever.' (Psalm 136:1)*

"*Read your Bible, pray every day, and you will grow, grow, grow.*" Truer words have never been penned. Take them to heart. This is my prayer for you as you commit to becoming an ardent student of your biblical bill of rights:

> *'For this reason we also, since the day we heard it, do not cease to pray for you, and to ask that you may be filled with the knowledge of His will in all wisdom and spiritual understanding: that you may walk worthy of the Lord, fully pleasing Him, being fruitful in every good work and increasing in the knowledge of God.' (Colossians 1:9-10)*

Chapter Seven

"True strength lies in submission which permits one to dedicate his life, through devotion, to something beyond himself."

Henry Miller

UNSTINTING DEDICATION TO GOD IS THE KEY

There is a generally held misconception amongst believers that God relates to all of His children in exactly the same way. This is principally because we have a perspective of God and His family as being some socialist type society where we are all equal and address each other as 'brother' and 'comrade.' Nothing could be further from the truth.

The Scripture we rely on to affirm this misguided belief is Acts 10:34 when Peter is speaking and he says, *"Most certainly and thoroughly I now perceive and understand that God shows no partiality and is no respecter of persons."* We conveniently forget verse 35 which reads, *"But in every nation he who venerates and has a reverential fear for God, treating Him with worshipful obedience and living uprightly, is acceptable to Him and sure of being received and welcomed by Him."*

I am not talking here about the love that God has for all of us. His love for us is unconditional—we could have never done anything to earn it. Neither am I talking about earning brownie points with God through performing 'religious' acts. But we must awaken to the reality that we all have a unique God given opportunity to develop our relationship with our Father and thereby discover more of His intricate character and ways. How eagerly you grasp and maximise this opportunity will distinguish you from others who maybe are not as keen to fully learn about God and draw closer to Him.

In the area of faith, we also know that although we all start out at the same level when we get saved, we don't all develop in our relationship with God at the same pace. Romans 12:3 makes it clear that we are all given **the same** measure of faith upon conversion. How then do you explain the great disparities in faith where some are able to develop their faith and do great exploits, and others remain stagnant and unproductive? Here are some examples of the different levels of faith:

No faith

> *'He said to them, "Why are you so timid and fearful? How is it that you have no faith?"' (Mark 4:40)*

Little faith

> *'Instantly, Jesus reached out His hand and caught and held him, saying to him, "O You of little faith, why did you doubt."' (Matthew 14:31)*

Great faith

> *'Then Jesus answered her, "O woman, great is your faith! Be it done for you as you wish."' (Matthew 15:28)*

> *'Now when Jesus heard this, He marvelled and said to those who were following, "Truly, I say to you, I have not found such great faith not even in Israel."'*

It is true that God is no respecter of persons. He affords us all the same opportunity to pursue Him regardless of our colour, our background, or our financial pedigree. But there are some who will pursue Him harder and more desperately than others, and it is these who will see receive more of Him.

> *"Behold I am coming quickly, and My reward is with Me to give to render to every man according to what he has done." (Revelation 22:12)*

It is your level of hunger and desperation for God that will determine the levels you go to in Him. Nobody can rise higher than their level of dedication to God. Some are willing to pay that price and others simply aren't.

> *"As the deer pants for the water brooks, so my soul pants for you O God. My soul thirsts for God, for the living God; when shall I come and appear before God?" (Psalm 42:1-2)*

Tragically for many, there are certain things that God will not be able to share with them, because He is all too aware that their dedication to Him is only superficial. Revelation knowledge belongs to the truly committed. Even in everyday life, we know that there are certain people that we cannot share privileged information with because we know that before the day ends they will have passed it on to other people. Companies have recipes, codes, and similar trade secrets that only a few are privileged to know, and disclose at their peril. Similarly in personal relationships, we entrust our spouses with information that we wouldn't dare share with anyone else. Secrets are only shared between lovers.

God is the same way. He has revelations concerning His power and ability that most of us will never discover because there is a cost to attaining them. It is the cost of unstinting dedication—a commitment to God that is deep and intense. One that is not based on only serving Him when He provides your creature comforts and everything is going well, but on being committed to Him when things are not going as you had hoped.

> *Though He slay me, yet I will trust Him (Job 13:15)*

It is being able to obey Him without question and trusting that because you only see in part and know in part, that He knows what is best for you.

> *'By faith Abraham, when he was called, obeyed by going out to a place which he was to receive for an inheritance, and he went out, not knowing where he was going.' (Hebrews 11:8)*

It is being able to sacrifice that which is dear to you, if He makes a demand on it.

> *'God said, "Take now your son, your only son Isaac, whom you love, and go to the region of Moriah; and offer him there as a burnt offering upon one of the mountains of which I will tell you." So Abraham rose early in the morning, saddled his donkey and took two of his young men with him and his son Isaac, and he split the wood for the burnt offering, and then began the trip to the place of which God had told him.' (Genesis 22:2-3)*

It is being willing to understand that there is a cost to pursuing God, and being willing to pay that cost.

> *'By faith, Moses when he had grown up, refused to be called the son of Pharaoh's daughter, choosing rather to suffer affliction with the people of God, than to enjoy the passing pleasures of sin, considering the reproach of Christ greater riches than the treasures of Egypt, for he was looking to the reward.' (Hebrews 11:24-25)*

It is becoming dead to self and alive only to God.

> *"I assure you, most solemnly, I tell you, unless a grain of wheat falls into the earth and dies, it remains alone; but if it dies, it produces many others and yields a rich harvest." (John 12:24)*

It is laying aside all our perceived privileges and advantages and recognising that it is only God's agenda that truly matters.

> *"But whatever things were gain to me, those things I have counted as loss for the sake of Christ. More than that, I count all things to be loss in view of the surpassing value of knowing Christ Jesus my Lord, for whom I have suffered the loss of all things, and*

count them but rubbish so that I may gain Christ."
(Philippians 3:7-8)

Is it any wonder then that the names of these individuals have gone down in the Faith Hall of Fame, and we speak of their exploits thousands of years after their deaths? Their dedication to God opened up a level of revelation that we are still feeding on today. The apostle Paul, despite not having physically walked with our Lord Jesus on the earth, had a level of revelation and insight that caused Apostle Peter to remark, *"just as also our beloved brother Paul, according to the wisdom given him, wrote to you, as also in all his letters, speaking in them of these things, in which are some things hard to understand . . ." (2 Peter 3:15-16)*

Some time ago, I heard Archbishop Enoch Adeboye make a statement that marked me permanently. He said, *"I can hear things that some of you cannot hear."* He was referring to divine signals and instructions from heaven that were not available to just anyone. There is a cost to receiving such levels of revelation.

> *'The secret things belong to the Lord our God, but those things which are revealed belong to us and to our children forever, that we may do all the words of this law.' (Deuteronomy 29:29)*

There remain great insights, ideas, inventions, strategies that are available to us if we tap into the very heartbeat of God. Once he reveals those things to us, they will not only benefit us, but become a legacy for our children and our children's children, forever and ever.

God loves nothing more than for His children to search Him out and pursue Him diligently. In God's economy you simply cannot get the 'deeper for the cheaper.'

> *'It is the glory of God to conceal a thing: but the honour of kings is to search out a matter.' (Proverbs 25:2)*

I was what I call a 'reluctant preacher.' I was none too enthused at the prospect of becoming a pastor because I had serious reservations about what it involved. From age 16 it was clear to many around me that there was a call of God upon my life, but I didn't want to have to deal with people on that level of intimacy, because I was all too aware of the deep scars that many people carried and the difficult situations I would have to minister to as a result. I didn't want anyone questioning my motives for being a preacher—whether I was in it for the money, and looking over all my possessions disdainfully and cynically, trying to establish whether I was fleecing my congregation. Like Jeremiah and Moses, I came up with all sorts of reasons not to do what the Lord was asking me to do. I didn't realize that because of this one act of disobedience, I was shutting myself off from God's goodness.

But the revelation hit me one day when I read the words of Paul, talking about Abraham:

> *'He staggered not at the promise of God through unbelief; but was strong in faith, giving glory to God; and being **fully persuaded** that, what he had promised, he was able also to perform.' (Romans 4:20-21)(emphasis mine)*

I got it. My faith could never produce on a high level until I was fully persuaded that God would be faithful to His promises. Today my confession every time before I preach is 'Thank you Lord for the privilege of serving your purposes in my generation.' Today, I am fully persuaded.

God is not in the business of revealing everything He knows to just anybody. Jesus when questioned by some of his followers as to why He spoke in Parables gave this stirring response on the sacredness of Kingdom truths:

> *'He said to them, "To you it has been given to come progressively to know, to recognize and understand more strongly and clearly the mysteries and secrets of the kingdom of God, but for others they are in parables, so that though looking, they may not see; and hearing, they may not comprehend." ' (Luke 8:10)*

God's secrets and mysteries aren't for everybody. But to take it a step further, they aren't just for you because you are a believer. You have to dedicate yourself to God, heart, body and soul, and only then will He reveal them to you.

When Nicodemus came to Jesus in the middle of the night with a burning question in his heart, he was all too aware that as much as he was a spiritual leader and a well respected authority in God's house, there were severe limitations on his understanding of God.

> *'The same came to Jesus by night, and said unto him,*
> *"Rabbi, we know that thou art a teacher come from*
> *God: for no man can do these miracles that thou doest,*
> *except God be with him.'" (John 3:2)*

Nicodemus was obviously intrigued by Jesus' undoubted anointing and all too aware of his own shortcomings. And Jesus graciously revealed to him the keys for how he too could walk in these same levels of power. The first step was that he needed to be born again.

> *'Jesus answered and said unto him, "Verily, verily, I*
> *say unto thee, Except a man be born again, he cannot*
> *see the kingdom of God.'" (John 3:3)*

Without being born again, all the ways of the Kingdom of God remain a mystery. That's why most of us can admit we used to think people who were saved were weird until we got saved ourselves, and realized that they had discovered a reality we were not part of because we were spiritually dead. Now being born again ourselves, we could 'see' for the first time that the Kingdom of God, or God's system was just as real as the world system we were used to.

But 'seeing' the Kingdom, according to Jesus was just the beginning.

> *'Jesus answered, "Verily, verily, I say unto thee, Except*
> *a man be born of water and of the Spirit, he cannot*
> *enter into the kingdom of God." (v5)*

'Entering' the Kingdom was clearly another level in God's economy. It was the difference between seeing what God was doing and understanding how and why He did it. When you are able to enter into God's kingdom through the divine power of revelation, you are able to enjoy the benefits of the kingdom that many others will only see from a distance.

> *'He made known his ways unto Moses, his acts unto the children of Israel.' (Psalm 103:7)*

When the Lord appeared to Samson's parents to inform them that they would give birth to the man who would deliver Israel from Philistine oppression, Manoah his father asked Him what His name was, to which the Lord replied, *"Why do you ask my name, seeing it is secret (wonderful)?"* *(Judges 13:18)* It was not for him to know that name. The prophet Isaiah however was given a revelation of that name over 700 years before Jesus was born into the earth.

> *'For unto us a child is born, unto us a son is given: and the government shall be upon his shoulder; and his name shall be called wonderful, Counsellor, the Mighty God, the everlasting Father, the Prince of Peace.' (Isaiah 9:6)*

When Job was in the middle of his tribulations, his friend Eliphaz began to remonstrate with him and essentially suggest that he was suffering his present torment as a result of his guilt. Job, knowing this was not the case, asked him, *"Were you present to hear the secret counsel of God?"* *(Job 15:8)*

Job was a dedicated lover of God, and he knew God's secrets. That is why he was not too impressed with what was essentially conjecture on Eliphaz's part. Job later begins to recall a time when because of his access to God's secrets, his life was blissful and sweet.

> *"Oh that I were as in months past, as in the days when God preserved me: When His candle shined upon my head, and when by His light I walked through darkness: As I was in the days of my youth, when the secret of God was upon my tabernacle: When the*

Almighty was yet with me, when my children were about me. When I washed my steps with butter, and the rock poured me out rivers of oil." (Job 29:2-6)

Paying the price in the area of dedication results in supernatural provision, divine direction and revelation in every area of your life which is dark. Something is only a mystery because we have darkness in that area. But once God gives us His insight, whether it is in the area of finances, marriage, or how to raise our children, we automatically become masters in that area. When the light appears, the darkness has to flee. Then we can experience the true freedom and pleasure He desires for us to enjoy.

'The secret of the Lord is with them that fear Him and He will show them His covenant. (Psalm 25:14)

Always remember that regardless of whatever may be going on in your life, there is always a way out. For you to experience freedom from fear and oppression, and deliverance from all your enemies, you have to be willing to pursue God as if your life depended on it, because in reality it does. When your desire is for Him and the things that matter to Him, then your deliverance is assured.

'One thing have I desired of the Lord, that will I seek. That I may dwell in the house of the Lord all the days of my life, to behold the beauty of the Lord, and to inquire in His temple. For in the time of trouble He shall hide me in His pavilion; in the secret place of His tabernacle He shall hide me. He shall set me high upon a rock. And now my head shall be lifted up above my enemies all around me." (Psalm 27:4-6)

Not only will you experience deliverance, but promotion will also visit your house when you are truly dedicated to God. Don't be deceived into thinking that you can live a careless, unguarded life and expect to discover the genuine freedoms that belong to you. You cannot spend your whole life in pursuit of temporal pleasure and expect for God to entrust you with his mysteries and secrets.

> *'For the perverse person is an abomination to the Lord, but his secret counsel is with the upright.' (Proverbs 3:32)*

God will entrust you with information that will have kings beating a path to your door. When Nebuchadnezzar had a dream which he could neither remember nor interpret, it was Daniel, the lover of God who was able to tell it to him.

> *'Daniel answered in the presence of the king, and said, "The secret which the king has demanded, the wise men, the astrologers, the magicians and the soothsayers cannot declare to the king. But there is a God in heaven who reveals secrets and He has made known to king Nebuchadnezzar what will be in the latter days."' (Daniel 2:27-28)*

> *'The king answered unto Daniel, and said, "Of a truth it is, that your God is a God of gods, and a Lord of kings, and a revealer of secrets, seeing thou couldst reveal this secret." Then the king made Daniel a great man, and gave him nay great gifts and made him ruler over the whole province of Babylon, and chief of the governors over all the wise men of Babylon.' (v47-48)*

When you are dedicated to God unequivocally, He makes it His business to guide you in all your ways. It is impossible then for you to not to succeed.

> *'And thine ears shall hear a word behind thee, saying, "This is the way, walk ye in it, when ye turn to the right hand, and when ye turn to the left."' (Isaiah 30:21)*

If you are tired of making decisions in the power of your own ability that never produce the results you hoped for, then make the one decision that can open up a whole new word of possibility for you. Get truly committed to God. Seek Him with all your heart. Then He will unveil your destiny to you in a grand way.

> *'Call to Me, and I will answer you, and show you great and mighty things, which you do not know.'*
> *(Jeremiah 33:3)*

Chapter Eight

SIN MAKES MINNOWS OF MEN

"There are two freedoms—the false, where a man is free to do what he likes; the true, where he is free to do what he ought."

Charles Kingsley

The concept of freedom is an interesting one because we all understand it differently. To some, freedom is the ability to do whatever they feel like doing. Many teenagers would probably tell you that freedom to them is being able to come and go as they please, and stay up late without having the burden of a curfew. When I was much younger I vowed that when I grew up I would eat as much ice cream as I could get my hands on, because I hated being limited to a few scoops at a time. That is what represented freedom to me. To someone else freedom is not having an overbearing boss breathing down your neck and watching your every move.

Maybe freedom to you is being able to go shopping without having to closely watch every penny you spend. Or being able to go on the holiday of your choice, instead of the budget holiday which is all you can afford at present. It could even be something as personal as being able to make your own decisions without always feeling undermined by those around you.

But whatever freedom means to you, it must always be remembered that freedom only finds its true expression within the parameters established by God. Doing anything outside of this puts you squarely in the realm of sin and anarchy. That's a tough message for today's society because we are part of a culture which believes that no one has the right to tell us what to do and that we are the only ones that have the right to decide what is right for us.

The late Samuel Hendel once said, *"The fact, in short, is that freedom, to be meaningful in an organized society must consist of an amalgam of hierarchy of freedoms and restraints."* There can be no true freedom without the accompanying restrictions on our behaviour.

True freedom is not the ability to do whatever you want. True freedom finds its greatest expression in God and in living out your liberties in line with what He would have you do.

> *'For you are free, yet you are God's slaves, so don't use your freedom as an excuse to do evil.' (1 Peter 2:15-17)*

That tells us that we are only really free when we are obeying God implicitly. He paid such a heavy price for us to even be able to exercise these freedoms.

> *'Who gave Himself on our behalf that He might redeem us, purchase our freedom from all iniquity and purify for Himself a people to be peculiarly His own, people who are eager and enthusiastic about living a life that is good and filled with beneficial deeds.' (Titus 2:14)*

Neither is freedom allowing our children to chart their own course independent of our guidance and instruction. Many psychologists today will encourage you to let your children decide for themselves what is right and wrong and establish their own moral compass, but the very idea of this is laughable. We are born into a fallen world with a sin nature that needs to be dealt with using God's Word, and if we fail to understand this, we are only setting ourselves up for a serious fall.

> *'Exclaiming, "Would that you had known personally, even at least in this your day, the things that make for peace (for freedom from all the distresses that are experienced as the result of sin and upon which your peace—your security, safety, prosperity, and*

happiness—depends)! But now they are hidden from your eyes.'" (Luke 19:42)

True freedom is understanding what Jesus did in delivering us from the clutches of sin and our fallen nature.

> *'Because God's children are human beings—made of flesh and blood—the Son also became flesh and blood. For only as a human being could he die, and only by dying could he break the power of the devil, who had the power of death. Only in this way could he set free all who have lived their lives as slaves to the fear of dying.' (Hebrews 2:14-15)*

Before Jesus went to the cross for us, we were subject to the devil's devices and were victims of sin, and we didn't have any control over the direction our lives took. We were effectively pawns in his hands. Sin is deceptive because it makes you believe that you are in control, when in reality the devil is pulling the strings and controlling you like a puppet. Sin invariably leads to death, and the only way to break free is through the God ordained process through salvation in Jesus Christ.

> *'For the wages of sin is death, but the gift of God is eternal life in Christ Jesus our Lord.' (Romans 6:23)*

God has bestowed on us such a wonderful gift of liberty. It is often the case however that as believers we use this gift as a licence to engage in behaviour that we have no business being involved in, because we feel we can abuse our privileges.

> *'For you, brethren, have been called to liberty; only do not use liberty as an opportunity for the flesh, but through love serve one another.' (Galatians 5:13)*

Sin will always result in bondage, but to hear some folk talk about it, sin is something trendy and exciting. We even applaud disobedience and rebellion in many of society's 'role models'. How many times do we see wild rockers being interviewed and everyone is in awe of their 'bad boy' image, as they smash up the stage and cuss out everyone with impunity?

When God speaks about our freedom and in the same breadth cautions us against the dangers of sin, it's not because He is trying to be a killjoy. Rather He knows all too well that whenever we sin, it destroys something within us. When Adam and Eve committed the first sin, the shame of what they had done caused them to hide from God.

> *'And they heard the sound of the LORD God walking in the garden in the cool of the day, and Adam and his wife hid themselves from the presence of the Lord God among the trees of the garden. Then the LORD God called to Adam and said to him, "Where are you?" So he said, "I heard Your voice in the garden, and I was afraid because I was naked; and I hid myself."' (Genesis 3:8-10)*

Sin will cause you to lose your confidence before God. When that happens you no longer have the guts to pursue your heavenly inheritance, but rather you end up just contenting yourself with temporary pleasure, and putting off any thoughts of God and what He has in store for you.

Sin puts you right back into the very thing that Jesus came to the earth to deliver you from. Sin will enslave you, and as much as you may think you are in control and having the time of your life, the reality is very much different.

> *'Do you not know that to whom you present yourselves slaves to obey, you are that one's slaves whom you obey, whether of sin leading to death, or of obedience leading to righteousness?' (Romans 6:16)*

Sin certainly has pleasure, nobody can deny that. If it didn't, the devil would have a hard time getting people to participate. The only problem is that the pleasure is very much a temporary release and afterwards the consequences will follow. The shame, depression, trauma and confusion that result far outweigh the supposed enjoyment.

Sin promises so much and yet in the end gives so little. There are millions of people worldwide who are bound by an addiction to pornography, alcohol, drug use or illicit sex. Rehab clinics are big business today. According to the Minnesota Institute for Public Health and drug prevention resource centre, 5,000 adults in the United States try cocaine for the first time each day. And a joint MSNBC, Stanford and Duquesne study reported that 25 million Americans visit cyber-sex sites between 1-10 hours per week, with 4.7 million viewing in excess of 11 hours per week.

In the UK the figures are no less alarming. In a 2009 Channel 4 survey, two thirds of 13-17 year olds said that they regularly viewed pornography. And figures released by the Office for National statistics showed a 6% increase in suicides between 2007 and 2008 from 5,377 to 5,706. It makes grim reading, but these statistics are just the tip of the iceberg. It is difficult to truly grasp the level of bondage that people in our societies are enduring.

All these 'recreational activities' seem so harmless when first tried out, but more often than not they result in a level of hopelessness and despair that beggars belief. The book of Proverbs, talking about the seductive nature of excessive wine, might as well be talking about the true nature of sin when it has run its full course.

> *'Those who linger long at the wine, those who go in search of mixed wine. Do not look on the wine when it is red, when it sparkles in the cup, when it swirls around smoothly; at the last it bites like a serpent, and stings like a viper.' (Proverbs 23:30-32)*

If you want to be truly free, you are going to have to be aware of the seductive nature of sin, and be willing to pay the price to stay out of its clutches. You are going to have to pay the price by crucifying your flesh and its natural desires, and choosing instead to pursue holiness because unless you do this you will never truly experience God's genuine freedom.

> *'Follow peace with all men, and holiness, without which no man shall see the Lord'. Hebrews 12:14)*

Will it be easy to do? I am not suggesting that it will be, but I am certainly saying that the rewards will be worth it, when you do. Someone once said that in life we pay one of two prices—the price of discipline or the price of regret. If we fail to discipline ourselves to live lives that fall in line with what God demands, then the day will come when we suffer the pain of regret, and the pain of knowing that we could have done more for God and become more in our time on the earth.

It really pains me when I see people at the end of their lives looking forlornly at the remains of what is left when they have abused their bodies with drugs and alcohol, and have left all their vitality in nightclubs which even charged them for the privilege. Knowing what God wanted them to become makes it even more painful to behold their downward spiral.

True freedom is found when we do our level best by the power of the Holy Spirit to live our lives in accordance with the Scriptures. Sure, we will have some difficult decisions to make along the way. But if we are committed to doing things God's way, we will reap the rewards that belong only to the righteous. We have to die to our preferences and let the purposes and will of God be established in our daily lives.

> *'I die daily.' (1 Corinthians 15:31)*

Are you involved in some secret sin right now and trying to figure out how you can break out of it? Believe me, I know how you feel, because I have been there. But you must realize that there is no way for you to come out of the throes of sin by yourself. You have to be willing to do it God's way. This is His guaranteed way of helping to deliver you:

> *'Awake to righteousness and sin not.' (1 Corinthians 15:34)*

When you open your eyes to, and become familiar with the privileged position you have in God through salvation, it will make you realize that you have power over sin. Once you are saved and receive God's righteousness as your own, you become a master over sin, instead of being its victim.

Sin makes us operate on a level that is so far below what God intended for us. But today as you renew your mind and appropriate God's promises as your own, you step right back into where you belong as a commander in life.

> *'Even so we, when we were children, were in bondage under the elements of the world. But when the fullness of the time had come, God sent forth His Son, born of a woman, born under the law, to redeem those who were under the law, that we might receive the adoption as sons. And because you are sons, God has sent forth the Spirit of His Son into your hearts, crying out, 'Abba, Father!' Therefore you are no longer a slave but a son, and if a son, then an heir of God through Christ.' (Galatians 4:3-7)*

Many continue to think that obeying God's Word puts you in a form of bondage, but Psalm 119 gives a different perspective:

> *'So shall I keep Your law continually, forever and ever. And I will walk at liberty, for I seek Your precepts.' (v44-45)*

It is both interesting and tragic to note how practising sin as a Believer will cause us to allow those who have no enduring covenant with our God to ride rough shod over us and rule us, and we start to think that's how things should be. However when God looks at this sorry scenario, He sees something unnatural and unbecoming.

> *'There is an evil I have seen under the sun, like an error which goes forth from the ruler—folly in set in many exalted places while rich men sit in humble places. I have seen slaves riding on horses and princes walking like slaves on the land.' (Ecclesiastes 10:5-7)*

It is not a new phenomenon. The children of Israel endured repeated captivity and torment from many different peoples whenever they strayed from obeying God and His commandments.

> *'But the Israelites did evil in the sight of the Lord, and the Lord gave them into the hand of Midian for seven years. They would encamp against them and destroy the crops as far as Gaza and leave no nourishment for Israel and no ox or sheep or donkey. And Israel was greatly impoverished because of the Midianites, and the Israelites cried to the Lord.' (Judges 6:1,4,6)*

Sin will make you subject to the oppressive whims of other men. Remember that the Midianites were descendants of Keturah, Abraham's concubine. They had no business troubling the children of Israel who were descended from Isaac—Abraham and Sarah's true progeny. It is the reason why as God's children we must depart from sin. Our entire inheritance is at stake.

Similarly, the Israelites endured captivity in Egypt for over four hundred years, before the Lord sent them a deliverer in the form of Moses.

> *'Now a new king arose over Egypt who did not know Joseph. He said to his people, "Behold, the people of the sons of Israel are more and mightier than we. Come let us deal wisely with them, or else they will multiply and in the event of war they will also join themselves to those who hate us, and fight against us and depart from the land." So they appointed taskmasters over them to afflict them with hard labour.'" (Exodus 1:8-11)*

I am reminded too of the terrorist tactics of the Midianites and how God having commissioned Gideon to deliver the Israelites, gave him a unique insight into the mindset of his oppressors.

> *'Now the same night it came about that the Lord said to him, "Arise, go down against the camp, for I have given it into your hands. But if you are afraid to go down, go with Purah your servant down to the camp, and you will hear what they say; afterward your hands will be strengthened that you may go down against*

*the camp." When Gideon came, behold a man was
relating a dream to his friend, And he said, "Behold
I had a dream; a loaf of barley bread was tumbling
into the camp of Midian, and it came to the tent and
struck it so that it fell, and turned it upside down
so that the tent lay flat." His friend replied, "This
is nothing less than the sword of Gideon, the son of
Joash, a man of Israel; God has given Midian and all
the camp into his hand." (Judges 6:9-14)*

When we decide to live in sin and rebellion, our covenant privileges will
be enjoyed by others and we will spend our days in want and lack and will
have to endure sickness, shame and embarrassment. But when we decide
to return wholeheartedly to God, He immediately restores our dignity and
our fortune.

*Lift up your eyes to the desolate heights and see: Where
have you not lain with men? By the road you have sat
for them like an Arabian in the wilderness and you
have polluted the land with your harlotries and your
wickedness. Therefore the showers have been withheld,
and there has been no latter rain. You have had a
harlot's forehead, you refuse to be ashamed. Will you
not from this time cry to Me, 'My Father, You are the
guide of my youth? Jeremiah 3:4-5)*

*"Return, O backsliding children," says the Lord "for
I am married to you. I will take you, one from a city
and two from a family, and I will bring you to Zion.
And I will give you shepherds according to My heart,
who will feed you with knowledge and understanding.
Then it shall come to pass, when you are multiplied
and increased in the land in those days," says the Lord,
"that they will say no more, 'The ark of the covenant
of the Lord.' It shall not come to mind, nor shall they
remember it, nor shall they visit it, nor shall it be
made anymore. (v14-16)*

Until we learn to deal with the strongholds in our minds that try to hold us captive to sin we will never be truly free. You can only go so far without dealing with this vital area. We have to begin to see ourselves as deliverers of others, instead of always being the ones needing deliverance. We have to see ourselves in the role of Jesus, perpetuating His purposes in the earth, because that is exactly how God sees us.

> *'The deliverers will ascend Mount Zion to judge the mountain of Esau, and the kingdom will be the Lord's.' (Obadiah 1:21)*

So we have a lot of work to do. We must refuse to give in to the lure of sin. Sin is no longer our master, Jesus is, but we must enforce our deliverance from sin by aggressively resisting its subtle overtures. It becomes even more urgent when we understand that the destinies of countless others are tied to your own. Unless you enforce your freedom in the area of sin, many others will never experience freedom in their own lives.

Confess your sin today and receive your freedom. Do not hide it and pretend that it doesn't exist, because to do so is simply deceive yourself. When you put it out in the open before God, then He is able to completely deliver you. Enjoy the fullness of the freedom that God purchased for you!

> *'He who covers his sins will not prosper, but whoever confesses and forsakes them will have mercy. (Proverbs 28:13)*

Chapter Nine

WHAT DO YOU STAND FOR?

*"Unless I am convicted by Scripture and plain
reason, I do not accept the authority of popes and
councils, for they have contradicted each other—my
conscience is captive to the Word of God. I cannot
and will not recant anything, for to go against
conscience is neither right nor safe. Here I stand, I
cannot do otherwise. God help me. Amen."*

Martin Luther

If there is one lesson I believe we all have to wholeheartedly take to heart, this is it. We have to continually remind ourselves of our responsibility as men and women of God to maintain the enduring virtues and values that Christ enjoined us to perpetuate. We must forcefully stand up for the freedoms we believe in, because to fail to do so will be to contribute to their eventual erosion.

I wonder what would happen if a seventeenth century individual could be transported through time and transplanted into the twenty first century. What would they see and experience? Forget the industrial, communication and technological advancements, which are phenomenal in themselves. I am talking about the virtues, or rather the lack of virtues that they would see. A generation that does not value the sanctity of marriage, or the value of telling the truth and keeping your word. A culture in which you are ridiculed and considered old fashioned for believing in God. A people who don't seem to have strong opinions about the things that really matter. Through his eyes, this is a bunch of people for whom anything goes.

Our generation will pursue a plethora of meaningless causes, revolving around the rights of trees and animals and yet fail to have any strong political or moral convictions. In the main we are content to be called Christians but when the rubber hits the road, we often refuse to take a righteous stance against much of the evil that is all around us.

The reason why this is so important is because the freedoms that our Lord purchased for us have to be enforced in our own lives. We have to make a determination to live our lives in such a way that the fruit of His sacrifice is evident for all to see.

> *"Either make the tree good, and his fruit good; or else make the tree corrupt, and his fruit corrupt: for the tree is known by his fruit. O generation of vipers, how can ye, being evil, speak good things? For out of the abundance of the heart the mouth speaks." (Matthew 12:33-34)*

The reason we have to be so militant in protecting these freedoms and standing up for what we believe, is because we have to consider not just the initial cost of obtaining those freedoms, but the efforts of the countless brave men and women who sacrificed so much to preserve them for us.

> *And what more shall I say? For the time would fail me to tell of Gideon and Barak and Samson and Jephthah, also of David and Samuel and the prophets who through faith subdued kingdoms, worked righteousness, obtained promises, stopped the mouths of lions, quenched the violence of fire, escaped the edge of the sword, out of weakness were made strong, became valiant in battle, turned to flight the armies of the aliens. Women received their dead raised to life again. Others were tortured, not accepting deliverance, that they might obtain a better resurrection. Still others had trial of mockings and scourgings, yes, and of chains and imprisonment. They were stoned, they were sawn in two, were tempted, were slain with the sword. They wandered about in sheepskins and goatskins, being destitute, afflicted, tormented—of whom the world was not worthy. They wandered in*

deserts and mountains, in dens and caves of the earth. And all these, having obtained a good testimony through faith, did not receive the promise, God having provided something better for us, that they should not be made perfect apart from us.

I often ask myself how many of us believers today would have the guts to stand up to a Nebuchadnezzar who is demanding that we bow down to his graven image, or else be thrown in a fiery furnace. Or how many, like Daniel, would ignore the evil plots of our enemies and pray openly to God when there were specific laws in place prohibiting that very thing, with the punishment being a short stint in a lions' den.

My heart goes out to the many Christians in countries all over the world who today are paying such a heavy price to enjoy many of the privileges we take for granted. They have to meet in secret, share bibles, be tortured for their beliefs, and even lose their lives. They have a wonderful reward waiting for them throughout eternity.

But even in everyday life, and in much less dramatic circumstances, we are constantly faced with making decisions that tell the world who we really are. Whether we realize it or not, the world is watching our every step and waiting for us to trip up and fall. We can't give them that satisfaction.

Compromise has crippled the Church of Jesus Christ. We have shamefully and dishonourably conceded our convictions on the twin altars of convenience and expedience. It is one of the reasons why our message is losing its edge. People who are on the outside looking in are seeing the exact same things they see in their own day to day lives and not the shining light that would draw them to our God. Something has to change, and fast.

In the book of Jeremiah, we are introduced to a group of people who took a stance on something that their forefather had warned them against.

'The word which came to Jeremiah from the Lord in the days of Jehoiakim the son of Josiah, king of Judah, saying," Go to the house of the Rechabites, speak to

them, and bring them into the house of the Lord, into one of the chambers, and give them wine to drink."'

'Then I set before the sons of the house of the Rechabites bowls full of wine, and cups; and I said to them, "Drink wine." But they said, "We will drink no wine, for Jonadab the son of Rechab, our father, commanded us, saying, 'You shall drink no wine, you nor your sons, forever. You shall not build a house, sow seed, plant a vineyard, nor have any of these; but all your days you shall dwell in tents, that you may live many days in the land where you are sojourners.' Thus we have obeyed the voice of Jonadab the son of Rechab, our father, in all that he charged us, to drink no wine all our days, we, our wives, our sons, or our daughters, nor to build ourselves houses to dwell in; nor do we have vineyard, field, or seed."' (Jeremiah 35:1-2, 5-9)

The Rechabites were so committed to their beliefs that they wouldn't compromise them for anything or anyone. God was impressed by their uncompromising stance, but had a stirring rebuke against the Israelites and their blasé attitude towards God.

'Thus says the Lord of hosts, the God of Israel: Go and tell the men of Judah and the inhabitants of Jerusalem, "Will you not receive instruction to obey My words?" says the Lord. "The words of Jonadab the son of Rechab, which he commanded his sons, not to drink wine, are performed; for to this day they drink none, and obey their father's commandment. But although I have spoken to you, rising early and speaking, you did not obey Me. (v14)

A life that is lived without convictions is truly a meaninghless life.

"There are always two choices. Two paths to take. One is easy. And its only reward is that it's easy." (Author Unknown)

You can either live the rest of your life on your knees in subjection to the standards, mindsets and opinions that are all around you, or you can decide to stand up for the things that God prizes. If you choose the path of least resistance you will never experience the very best God has to offer you, because He always rewards those who hold onto His Word.

> *'Then the children of Judah came to Joshua in Gilgal. And Caleb the son of Jephunneh the Kenizzite said to him: "You know the word which the Lord said to Moses the man of God concerning you and me in Kadesh Barnea. I was forty years old when Moses the servant of the Lord sent me from Kadesh Barnea to spy out the land, and I brought back word to him as it was in my heart. Nevertheless my brethren who went up with me made the heart of the people melt, but I wholly followed the Lord my God. So Moses swore on that day, saying, 'Surely the land where your foot has trodden shall be your inheritance and your children's forever, because you have wholly followed the Lord my God.' And now, behold, the Lord has kept me alive, as He said, these forty-five years, ever since the Lord spoke this word to Moses while Israel wandered in the wilderness; and now, here I am this day, eighty-five years old. As yet I am as strong this day as on the day that Moses sent me; just as my strength was then, so now is my strength for war, both for going out and for coming in.*
>
> *Now therefore, give me this mountain of which the Lord spoke in that day; for you heard in that day how the Anakim were there, and that the cities were great and fortified. It may be that the Lord will be with me, and I shall be able to drive them out as the Lord said."*
> *And Joshua blessed him, and gave Hebron to Caleb the*

> *son of Jephunneh as an inheritance. Hebron therefore became the inheritance of Caleb the son of Jephunneh the Kenizzite to this day, because he wholly followed the Lord God of Israel. (Joshua 14:6-14)*

Your inheritance is tied to your willingness to stand on the Word of God and the promises of God. It may often seem like others who do not share your passion for and commitment to God are winning. But always remember that we are fast approaching the day when we will all stand before our Creator to give an account for the decisions we made while in this body. In that day, every sacrifice will be worth it, every commitment to God's word of inestimable value. Don't be double minded in your Christian walk. Not only will you not be rewarded for it, but you will also never locate the true heartbeat of God.

> *'Such doubters are thinking two different things at the same time, and they cannot decide about anything they do. They should not think they will receive anything from the Lord.' (James 1:8)*

I leave you with the rousing story of Eric Liddell, a man who understood the value of standing uncompromisingly for what he believed in.

Eric was born in China to Scottish missionaries. Eric Liddell loved the Lord and wanted to honour him with the life he had been given. He was the fastest runner in all of Scotland and won race after race. He knew that God had given the ability to run fast and so in 1924 he entered the Paris Olympics. The whole country was excitedly waiting for him to compete in the 100 metre sprint and he was expected to win a gold medal.

However a conflict quickly became apparent. The time trials for Eric's race were to be held on a Sunday, and because of his desire to keep the Sabbath holy, Eric refused to race on Sundays, electing to keep the day free for worship and rest. The Scottish nation was outraged and Eric quickly fell out of favour. Notwithstanding the public outcry and accompanying pressure, Eric stuck to his guns and refused to compromise.

Eventually a solution was found. The Olympic committee agreed to allow Eric to compete in two other events, which did not take place on a Sunday: the 200-meter and the 400-metre races. Though he faced tough competition and was somewhat out of his league in these events, Eric surprised the world with a gold medal win and new world record in the 400m and a Bronze in the 200m. Eric returned as a national hero and used his subsequent speaking engagements to share his faith.

After his running days came to an end, Eric enrolled at the Scottish Congregational College in Edinburgh to pursue his goal of becoming a missionary. In 1925 he returned to China with his wife and for the better part of 20 years they served as missionaries. With the horrors of World War II all around them, they continued to share their faith and be a witness for God even when interned in a Japanese concentration camp. In 1945, Eric died in the camp of a malignant tumour. The news of his death touched all of Scotland. His achievements were immortalised in the 1980's film 'Chariots of Fire.'

> *"Them that honour me, I will honour, and those who despise me shall be lightly esteemed." (1 Samuel 2:30)*

Printed in Great Britain
by Amazon

43978167R00061